高等职业院校单招考试用书

英 语

主 编 韩彦林 王 静
副主编 柳丽苗 刘贝贝

北京理工大学出版社
BEIJING INSTITUTE OF TECHNOLOGY PRESS

版权专有　侵权必究

图书在版编目（CIP）数据

英语 / 韩彦林，王静主编．－－北京：北京理工大学出版社，2021.9

高等职业院校单招考试用书

ISBN 978－7－5763－0424－4

Ⅰ．①英… Ⅱ．①韩…②王… Ⅲ．①英语课－高等职业教育－入学考试－自学参考资料 Ⅳ．①G634.413

中国版本图书馆 CIP 数据核字（2021）第 195130 号

出版发行 / 北京理工大学出版社有限责任公司
社　　址 / 北京市海淀区中关村南大街 5 号
邮　　编 / 100081
电　　话 / （010）68914775（总编室）
　　　　　（010）82562903（教材售后服务热线）
　　　　　（010）68944723（其他图书服务热线）
网　　址 / http：//www.bitpress.com.cn
经　　销 / 全国各地新华书店
印　　刷 / 三河市天利华印刷装订有限公司
开　　本 / 787 毫米×1092 毫米　1/16
印　　张 / 11.25　　　　　　　　　　　　　　责任编辑 / 武丽娟
字　　数 / 254 千字　　　　　　　　　　　　　文案编辑 / 武丽娟
版　　次 / 2021 年 9 月第 1 版　2021 年 9 月第 1 次印刷　责任校对 / 刘亚男
定　　价 / 58.00 元　　　　　　　　　　　　　责任印制 / 施胜娟

图书出现印装质量问题，请拨打售后服务热线，本社负责调换

前　言

2021年6月15日，教育部办公厅等六部门联合下发关于做好2021年高职扩招专项工作的通知，这是继2019年以来，连续三年下发高职扩招专项考试招生工作的通知，从这一点上，就能够看出来国家大力发展高职教育的推行力度。大力发展高职教育，不但是国家政策，而且是发展趋势。高职教育大规模发展，高职学生会越来越多，相应的，高职入学考试的竞争也会越来越大。相对于普通高考而言，目前单招考试是中职学生的最佳选择，所以，单招考试的人数每年都在大幅度增加，竞争也一年比一年激烈。为了帮助单招考生全面、系统、科学、高效地复习英语课程，把握高职单招英语考试的最新动向，有效提高考试成绩，编者在总结多年单招辅导经验基础之上，根据历年来单招考试规律及考试大纲要求，编写了这本单招考试辅导实用教材，以帮助广大单招考生顺利通过高职入学考试。

本教材有以下几个鲜明的特点：

第一，实用性强。本教材由多年辅导单招考试学生的一线教师根据亲身教学经验编写，具有非常强的实用性，很多内容属于"独门秘籍"，对考生快速提高成绩行之有效。

第二，专业性强。本教材在分析历年单招考试试题和科学预判考试趋向的基础上给考生提供了最专业的复习指导，教材的每个章节都有知识讲解、真题分析和实战演练。

第三，针对性强。本教材针对河北省单招考生进行编写，能够衔接中职的文化课程，符合河北省单招考生的实际水平，可以满足考生的应考需要。

第四，资料最新。本教材体现了三个"新"：一是"思路新"。编写思路简洁明快，让考生用最短的时间，掌握最多的知识，取得最好的成绩。二是"材料新"。教材中很多试题材料选用的都是新鲜素材，特别加入了近几年单招考试真题。三是"日期新"。当前国内图书市场上单招考试辅导教材种类很多，但有很多是多年前编写的，早就不适应目前的单招考试形势，本教材则是最新的教材，它紧跟单招考试政策，紧抓单招重点内容，实用价值非常大。

因为编写时间仓促，教材中如有疏漏和不妥之处，恳请广大读者批评指正。

编　者

目 录

第一章 基础知识 1
  第一节 名词 1
  第二节 冠词 7
  第三节 代词 11
  第四节 形容词 21
  第五节 副词 28
  第六节 数词 33
  第七节 介词 42
  第八节 连词 46
  第九节 动词 52
  第十节 动词时态 58
  第十一节 动词语态 68
  第十二节 非谓语动词 72
  第十三节 句子的基本句型 83
  第十四节 状语从句 87
  第十五节 名词性从句 99
  第十六节 定语从句 105
  第十七节 感叹句 110
  第十八节 倒装句 113
  第十九节 主谓一致 117

第二章 专项练习 125
  第一节 日常交际用语 125
  第二节 完形填空 134
  第三节 阅读理解 144

第三章　模拟测试 ……………………………………………………………………… 158
　　模拟测试（一） ……………………………………………………………………… 158
　　模拟测试（二） ……………………………………………………………………… 161
　　模拟测试（三） ……………………………………………………………………… 165
参考答案 ………………………………………………………………………………… 169

第一章 基础知识

第一节 名词

一、名词的定义

名词（noun 简称 n.）是表示人、事物、地点、现象及其他抽象概念等名称的词。

二、名词的分类

从形式上进行分类，英语名词可以划分成普通名词和专有名词两大类。普通名词是一类人或东西或是一个抽象概念的名词，如：book，sadness 等。专有名词是某个（些）人、地方、机构等专有的名称，如 Beijing，China 等。

从意义上进行分类，英语名词可分为个体名词、集体名词、物质名词和抽象名词四类。个体名词表示某类人或东西中的个体，如：pen，car。集体名词表示若干个个体组成的集合体，如：family，people。物质名词表示无法分为个体的实物，如：air，meat。抽象名词表示动作、状态、品质、感情等抽象概念，如：work，love。

从可数和不可数来看，个体名词可以用数目来计算，称为可数名词。物质名词和抽象名词无法用数目来计算，称为不可数名词。集体名词有的可数，有的不可数。

(一) 普通名词

普通名词指一类人或事物的名称。英语中普通名词分为可数名词和不可数名词。可数名词一般有单、复数两种形式，如 a/one child，ten children。不可数名词一般只有一种形式，如 water。不可数名词之前不可直接用泛指限定词和数词。不可数名词可与 some 一起用，如：some money，some water；也可与 the 一起用，如 the information。

1. 可数名词及其复数形式。

（1）可数名词的复数形式一般由词尾加-s 或-es 构成，其规则如下：

一般情况加-s 在清辅音后读/s/ maps，books

在浊辅音及元音后读/z/ cars，photos

在/t/后读/ts/ cats，students

在/d/后读/dz/ beds，guards

在/dʒ/后读/iz/ bridges，ages

（2）以字母 s，x，ch，sh 结尾的词加-es 读/iz/ classes，brushes。

（3）以辅音字母+y 结尾的词将 y 改成 i，加-es 读/z/ factories，stories。

（4）以字母 o 结尾的词一般加-s 读/z/ zoos, pianos, photos。
但 heroes, negroes, tomatoes, potatoes 加 es
（5）以字母 f 或 fe 结尾的词一般加-s 读/s/ roofs, chiefs。
少数将 f, fe 改为-ves 读/z/ shelves, knives, leaves

2. 可数名词复数形式的不规则构成法。

英语中有一部分名词由于历史或词源原因其复数形式的构成法是不规则的。这种情况主要有：

（1）元音字母变化。

例如：foot-feet   man-men   woman-women
       tooth-teeth   goose-geese   mouse-mice

（2）结尾为-en。

例如：child-children

（3）单复数同形。

单复数同形的名词主要有：

sheep, fish, Chinese, Japanese, deer 等。

（4）只有复数形式。

trousers, glasses（眼镜）, clothes, goods 若表达具体数目，要借助量词 pair（对，双）; suit（套）。

例如：a pair of glasses; two pairs of trousers

（5）集体名词，以单数形式出现，但实为复数。

people, police, cattle 等本身就是复数，不能说 a people, a police, a cattle, 但可以说 a person, a policeman, a head of cattle。

the English, the British, the French, the Chinese, the Japanese, the Swiss 等名词，表示国民总称时，作复数用。

如：The Chinese are industrious and brave. 中国人民是勤劳勇敢的。

（6）以 s 结尾，仍为单数的名词。

例如：

a. maths, politics, physics 等学科名词，为不可数名词，是单数。

b. news 是不可数名词。

c. the United States, the United Nations 应视为单数。

The United Nations was organized in 1945. 联合国是 1945 年组建起来的。

d. 以复数形式出现的书名、剧名、报纸、杂志名也可视为单数。

"*The Arabian Nights*" is a very interesting story-book.

《一千零一夜》是一本非常有趣的故事书。

3. 不可数名词。

不可数名词的用法特征主要有以下几种：

（1）不带冠词的单数形式需用动词单数作谓语。

Knowledge is power. 知识就是力量。

（2）由 much, little 等词修饰。

They have saved much money for future use.
他们存了很多钱以备未来使用。

（3）与表示单位的量词如 a piece of 等连用。

Go and fetch me a piece of chalk. 给我拿一支粉笔。

要十分注意的是：不可数名词不能与不定冠词或数词直接用在一起，如不能说 a good news，an advice，a hard work 等。

不可数名词可以与量词使用构成不同的词组：

例如：a piece of paper 一张纸

　　　a drop of water 一滴水

　　　a loaf of bread 一条面包

　　　a bag of money 一袋钱

　　　a bottle of milk 一瓶牛奶

　　　a pair of shoes 一双鞋

（二）专有名词

专有名词用来指具体的人、地点、日子或物体的名称。其特点是：第一个字母大写，通常不与冠词连用，无复数形式。

1. 人名。

英美人的姓名与中国人的姓名恰恰相反，姓在后面，名在前面，姓名前通常不用冠词。

Mary Smith；George Washington

（1）一般熟人间通常用名称呼。

How's John getting on? 约翰近来好吗？

（2）在不熟悉的人之间或表示礼貌时，常把姓和称谓连用。

Would you please tell John Smith to come to the office?

请你告诉约翰·史密斯到办公室来好吗？

（3）姓氏复数前加定冠词可表示全家人。

The Turners have gone to America. 特纳一家人去美国了。

2. 地名。

（1）大部分单数形式的地名不用定冠词。

Asia；America；China；London；Shanghai

（2）大部分单数形式的湖、岛、山名前不加定冠词。

Qinghai Lake；Mount Tai

（3）山脉、群岛、海洋、河流、运河、海湾、海峡、半岛、沙漠名前一般加定冠词。

the Pacific；the English Channel；the Sahara

3. 日期名。

（1）节日名前通常不用冠词。Christmas；National Day

（2）星期名前通常不用冠词。Sunday；Tuesday

（3）月份名前通常不用冠词。April；December

三、名词所有格

名词所有格是指一个名词与另一个名词之间存在所有关系时所用的形式。其构成有两种：一种是由名词末尾加's构成；另一种由介词 of 加名词构成。前者多用来表示有生命的东西；后者多用来表示无生命的东西。

Children's Palace 少年宫
Tom's bike 汤姆的自行车
the title of the book 书名
the legs of the table 桌子的腿

（一）所有格形式的构成

1. 单数名词后加's，其读音与名词复数结尾的读音相同。
the girl's father 女孩的父亲
2. 以 s 结尾的复数名词后加'。
two hours' walk 两个小时的步行
3. 不以 s 结尾的复数名词后加's。
Children's Day 儿童节
4. 以 s 结尾的人名，可以加's，也可加'。
Thomas's brother 托马斯的兄弟
Charles' job 查尔斯的工作
5. 表示各自的所有关系，不是共有的，则要分别在名词末尾加's。
John's and Mary's rooms 约翰和玛丽各人的房间
若表示共有的，则在最后一个名词的末尾加's
John and Mary's room 约翰和玛丽合住的房间

（二）'s 所有格的用法

's 所有格常表示有生命的东西，但也可表示无生命的东西。

1. 表示时间。
Today's newspaper 今天的报纸
2. 表示自然现象。
the moon's rays 月光
3. 表示国家、城市机构。
Shanghai's industry 上海的工业
4. 表示度量衡及价值。
twenty dollars' value 20 美元的价值
five miles' distance 5 英里的距离

真题分析

1. You may go to the _____ if you want to buy vegetables.
   A. supermarket   B. library   C. theatre   D. bookshop

分析：如果你想要买蔬菜，你可以去超市。A. 超市；B. 图书馆；C. 剧院；D. 书店。选项中只有超市有蔬菜卖。故选 A。

2. —What would you like to eat?
   —Some _____, please.
   A. bread　　　　B. cake　　　　C. coffee　　　　D. tea

   分析：——你想要吃什么？——请来一些面包。bread 面包；cake 蛋糕；coffee 咖啡；tea 茶；根据 What would you like to eat? 可知此处介绍吃的食物，有 some 修饰，故此处用 bread 或 cakes，但 B 选项 cake 是单数，故选 A。

3. —Look! They are _____.
   —Yes. We are proud of them.
   A. man scientist　　　　　　　　　B. women scientists
   C. woman scientists　　　　　　　D. man scientists

   分析：——看！她们是女科学家。——是的。我们为她们感到骄傲。英文中当 man, woman 修饰名词复数时 man/woman 和所修饰名词都要变成复数，故选 B。

4. June 1st is _____ Day. All the children enjoy it very much.
   A. the Childrens'　　B. Children's　　C. Childrens'　　D. the Children's

   分析：英语中表示节日时，前面不能用定冠词 the，故排除 A 和 D；因为 children 本身就是复数，其名称所有格应该是加's，故用 Children's。所以本题选 B。

5. —How many foreign workers are there in your company?
   —There are five, three _____ and two _____.
   A. German；Frenchman　　　　　　B. Germans；Frenchmen
   C. Germany；French　　　　　　　D. Germany；Frenchmen

   分析：你的公司有多少个外国工作人员呢？有 5 个，3 个德国人，2 个法国人。German 德国人，复数形式为直接加 s，Frenchman 的复数形式为 Frenchmen，故选 B。

实战演练

(　) 1. Tom is reading a _____.
　　　　A. chess　　B. ball　　　C. game　　　D. book

(　) 2. I'm a little hungry now. I only drank some _____ before I came to school.
　　　　A. apple　　B. milk　　　C. banana　　D. noodle

(　) 3. Please give me some _____ on how to spend the coming weekend.
　　　　A. space　　B. advice　　C. praise　　D. courage

(　) 4. —I'm thirsty. Could you get me something to drink?
　　　　—Sure. Here's some _____, please.
　　　　A. bread　　B. meat　　　C. water　　　D. kite

(　) 5. _____ are going to pick you up tomorrow morning.
　　　　A. Smith　　B. The Smith　　C. The Smiths　　D. Mr. Smith

(　) 6. Listen! Can you hear a girl's _____?
　　　　A. noise　　B. voice　　C. sound　　　D. noises

(   ) 7. He has three _____ under the bed.
　　A. pair of shoes　　　　　　B. pairs of shoes
　　C. pairs of shoe　　　　　　D. shoes

(   ) 8. —Did you enjoy the _____ ?
　　—Yes, it was delicious.
　　A. party　　B. trip　　　　C. meal　　　　D. movie

(   ) 9. After four _____ work, Tom was too tried to move.
　　A. days　　B. days'　　　　C. day's　　　　D. day

(   ) 10. Here is _____ for you.
　　A. a good news　　　　　　B. a piece of good news
　　C. so good news　　　　　　D. many good news

(   ) 11. This is _____ ball, you should return it to him.
　　A. the boys　B. the boy　　C. the boy's　　D. the boys'

(   ) 12. There isn't _____ in the bottle.
　　A. a lot of waters　　　　　B. many water
　　C. much water　　　　　　　D. much waters

(   ) 13. June 1st is _____ Day.
　　A. Children's　　　　　　　B. Children
　　C. Child　　　　　　　　　D. Children'

(   ) 14. These books are _____ .
　　A. Lucy and Lily　　　　　　B. Lucy and Lily's
　　C. Lucy's and Lily's　　　　　D. Lucy's and Lily

(   ) 15. We met some _____ in Shanghai last year.
　　A. Japaneses　　　　　　　B. the Japanese
　　C. Japanese　　　　　　　　D. Japan

(   ) 16. There _____ five minutes left.
　　A. are　　B. has　　　　　C. have　　　　D. is

(   ) 17. Please pass me some _____ .
　　A. tomato and potato　　　　B. tomatoes and potatoes
　　C. tomatoes and potato　　　D. tomato and potatoes

(   ) 18. Where are _____ ?
　　A. the teachers' rooms　　　B. the teacher's rooms
　　C. the teacher's room　　　　D. the room of the teacher

(   ) 19. The _____ is made of _____ .
　　A. houses, glass　　　　　　B. house, glasses
　　C. house, glass　　　　　　　D. houses, glasses

(   ) 20. Everyone knows that _____ love to eat _____ .
　　A. cat, mouse　　　　　　　B. cats, mice
　　C. cats, mouse　　　　　　　D. cat, mice

第二节 冠词

一、冠词的定义

冠词（article）是一种辅助性的词，在句中不独立担任一个成分，放在名词前，帮助说明名词的含义。冠词有不定冠词（a, an）和定冠词（the）两种。a 和 an 的基本含义是"一，一个"，表示泛指，不强调数目观念，只表示名词不是特定的；the 的基本含义是"这个，那个"，表示特指，在可数的单复数名词或不可数名词前面都可以用。

二、冠词的基本用法

（一）不定冠词

不定冠词用 a 还是 an 由后面一个词的首音（不是辅音字母）决定。以元音开头的词前用 an，以辅音（不是元音字母）开头的词前用 a。例如：

元音开头：an apple, an egg, an elephant, an opera, an umbrella, an hour

辅音开头：a tree, a university, a house, a European country, a one-eyed man

值得注意的是：

1. 如果不定冠词后面第一个词以元音字母 u 开头就用 a。

a university, a unit, a uniform, a useless book, a useful animal

2. 如果不定冠词后面第一个词以不发音的字母 h 开头，而 h 后面第一个音的音素是元音因素，就用 an。an hour, an honest man。

3. 如果不定冠词和名词前有其他词，不定冠词的形式仍取决于它后面第一个词的语音形式。例如 an old actress, a beautiful actress。

不定冠词的用法如下：

1. 用在单数可数名词前，表示一类人或事物。

A dictionary is a useful book.

词典是一本有用的书。

An underground train can start and stop quickly.

地铁开得快，停得快。

2. 说明某人或某东西属于哪一类。

This is a book.

这是一本书。

He used to be an engineer.

他过去是个工程师。

3. 泛指某人或某物，但未具体说明何人、何物。

A boy is waiting for me.

一个男孩在等我。

Give me a pen, please.

请给我一支钢笔。

4. 表示数量，有"一"的意思。

Behind the house there is a garden.

房子后面有一个花园。

He often goes home once a week.

他经常一周回家一次。

5. 用于某些固定词组中。

a few, a little, a lot of, a number of, just a minute, in a hurry, for a while, for a long time, a cup of, a bottle of, have a rest, have a talk, have a fever, have a good time, have（take）a walk, have a toothache, take a bath, give a lesson

（二）定冠词

定冠词的用法如下：

1. 指彼此都知道的人或事物。

Open the door, please. Go and close the window.

请把门打开。去把窗户关上。

2. 特指某（些）人或某（些）事物。

The girl in red is my sister.

穿红衣服的女孩是我妹妹。

The man over there is our English teacher.

那边的那个人是我们的英语老师。

The book on the desk is mine.

桌子上的书是我的。

3. 指前面提到过的人或事物。

Here is a picture of a modern car factory.

这是一张现代汽车厂的照片。

My father works in the factory.

我父亲在这家工厂工作。

4. 用在序数词和形容词最高级前，在方位词前。

The Nile is the longest river in the world.

尼罗河是世界上最长的河流。

He won the first prize.

他得了一等奖。

The sun rises in the east.

太阳从东方升起。

5. 用在某些名词化的形容词、过去分词前，表示一类人或事物。

the rich 富人

the sick 病人

6. 用在某些专用名词前。

the Great Wall 长城

the People's Republic of China 中华人民共和国

the United Nations 联合国

the Netherlands 荷兰

7. 用在江河、海洋、山脉、湖泊、群岛的名称的前面。

the North China Plain 华北平原

the Rocky Mountains 落基山脉

the Yangtse River 长江

8. 用在一些短语中。

in the morning（/afternoon/evening），in the day，by the way，on the whole，the next morning，all the year around，the other day，at the same time

（三）不用冠词的情况

1. 在一些专有名词前，如：China，Beihai Park。

2. 名词前面已有用作定语的 this，that，my，your，some，any 等代词前。如：

The letter is from my father.

这封信是我父亲寄来的。

I have a book in my hand.

我手里有一本书。

3. 在复数名词表示一类人或事物前。如：

Horses are useful animals. 马是有用的动物。

I like cakes. 我喜欢蛋糕。

4. 在节日名称、称呼语和表示官衔的名词前以及星期、月份、季节前。如：

Today is Sunday. 今天是星期天。

Spring is the best season in the year. 春天是一年中最好的季节。

June 1st is Children's Day. 6月1日是儿童节。

5. 在某些固定搭配和习惯用语中。如：

go to school 去上学

be in hospital 在医院

be in prison 在监狱

6. 一天三餐、球类运动的名称前。如：

I like to play basketball.

我喜欢打篮球。

We have lunch at school.

我们在学校吃午饭。

真题分析

1. Mr. Brown has _____ eight-year-old daughter. She is very lovely.

   A. a   B. an   C. the   D. /

   分析：Mr. Brown 有一个8岁大的女儿，非常可爱。eight-year-old 以元音因素/ei/开头，故用 an 修饰；a 修饰以辅音因素开头的单数名词；定冠词 the 表示特指，均不符题意，故选 B。

2. _____ bridge was built in _____ Ming Dynasty.
   A. a; a B. the; the C. a; the D. the; a

   分析：这座桥建于明朝。根据句子的语境，bridge 是指具体某一座桥，属特指，故用 the；某个朝代的前面要用 the。故选 B。

3. The cakes are delicious. He'd like to have _____ third one because _____ second one is rather too small.
   A. a; a B. the; the C. a; the D. the; a

   分析：蛋糕很可口。他想再吃一个，因为第二个蛋糕太小了。第一空的序数词前面加不定冠词表示"再一，又一"；第二空特指第二个蛋糕，要用定冠词。故选 C。

4. _____ boy in a black hat is my brother. He often plays _____ chess with my friends.
   A. A; the B. The; / C. The; a D. A; /

   分析：那个戴黑帽子的男孩是我的弟弟，他经常和我的朋友下棋。第一个空，说话双方都知道的名词前用定冠词 the；第二个空，play + 棋类，中间不加冠词，play chess 下棋；故选 B。

5. We have three meals _____ day. And we usually have _____ breakfast at 8:00 every morning.
   A. a, the B. a, a C. a, / D. /, the

   分析：我们一天吃三顿饭，我们通常每天早上八点吃早饭。three meals a day，一天三顿饭，固定搭配；吃早饭用 have/eat breakfast，固定搭配，故选 C。

实战演练

( ) 1. There is _____ "h" in _____ word "photo."
   A. a, a B. an, the C. the, an D. an, an

( ) 2. He goes to school after _____ breakfast.
   A. / B. the C. an D. a

( ) 3. There is _____ old bike. _____ old bike is Mr Zhao's.
   A. an; The B. the; An C. a; The D. the; The

( ) 4. _____ apple a day keeps the doctors away.
   A. The B. A C. An D. Two

( ) 5. At that time Tom was _____ one-year-old baby.
   A. a B. an C. the D. /

( ) 6. We can't see _____ sun at _____ night.
   A. the; the B. the; / C. a; / D. /; /

( ) 7. _____ useful book it is!
   A. What an B. How a C. What a D. What

( ) 8. She has _____ orange skirt. _____ skirt is nice.
   A. a; The B. an; The C. an; a D. the; The

(   ) 9. Beijing is _____ beautiful city. It's _____ capital of China.
   A. a; a　　　　B. the; the　　　　C. /; the　　　　D. a; the

(   ) 10. The museum is quite far. It will take you half _____ hour to get there by _____ bus.
   A. an; /　　　　B. an; a　　　　C. a; /　　　　D. /; /

(   ) 11. —When will _____ car race begin?
   —I'm not sure. Maybe next week, or maybe _____ week after next.
   A. a; the　　　　B. an; the　　　　C. the; a　　　　D. the; the

(   ) 12. Jenny often goes to play _____ basketball after class.
   A. a　　　　B. an　　　　C. the　　　　D. /

(   ) 13. — How long does it take us to go to Beijing from here?
   — It takes us _____ hour and a half to go to Beijing by _____ train.
   A. an; /　　　　B. a; the　　　　C. an; a　　　　D. an; the

(   ) 14. My uncle has two children, a son and a daughter. The son is _____ English teacher and _____ daughter is a doctor.
   A. a; the　　　　B. the; an　　　　C. the; a　　　　D. an; the

(   ) 15. John is _____ university student.
   A. /　　　　B. the　　　　C. an　　　　D. a

(   ) 16. These tables are made of _____ wood.
   A. /　　　　B. the　　　　C. an　　　　D. a

(   ) 17. I heard somebody playing _____ piano in _____ next room.
   A. an; /　　　　B. an; a　　　　C. a; /　　　　D. the; the

(   ) 18. There's _____ dictionary on _____ desk by your side.
   A. an; /　　　　B. an; a　　　　C. a; the　　　　D. /; the

(   ) 19. I often watch _____ TV in _____ evening.
   A. an; /　　　　B. an; a　　　　C. a; the　　　　D. /; the

(   ) 20. His mother told him to take _____ medicine three times _____ day.
   A. the; a　　　　B. an; a　　　　C. a; the　　　　D. /; the

第三节　代词

一、代词的定义

代词（pronoun 简称 pron.），是指代名词或一句话的一种词类。大多数代词具有名词和形容词的功能。英语中的代词，按其意义、特征及在句中的作用分为：人称代词、物主代词、反身代词、相互代词、指示代词、疑问代词、关系代词、不定代词和连接代词。

二、人称代词

人称代词是表示"我""你""他""她""它""我们""你们""他们"的词。

人称代词有人称、数和格的变化，见表1：

表1　人称代词变化

项目	单数		复数	
	主格	宾格	主格	宾格
第一人称	I	me	we	us
第二人称	you			
他	he	him	they	them
她	she	her		
它	it			
不定	one		ones	

如：He is my friend. 他是我的朋友。

It's me. 是我。

人称代词可用作主语、表语、宾语以及介词宾语。

I am a worker, and I work in the factory.

我是一个工人，我在工厂工作。

You are a good teacher.

你是一位优秀教师。

She is a little girl.

她是一个小女孩。

It's a heavy box, and I can't carry it.

这是一个重盒子，我搬不动。

Don't tell him about it.

不要告诉他这件事情。

She is always ready to help us.

她随时都在准备帮助我们。

Our teacher is very strict with us.

我们的老师对我们很严格。

人称代词中几个注意的情况：

第一人称单数代词"I（我）"不论在什么地方都要大写。

I study English every day. 我天天学习英语。

"we"常常代替"I"表示一种同读者、听众或观众之间的亲密关系。

We shall do our best to help the poor.

我们将尽全力帮助贫困者。

"she"常常代替国家、城市、宠物等，表示一种亲密或爱抚的感情。

I live in China. She is a great country.

我住在中国，她是一个伟大的国家。

"it"可指未确定身份的人、天气、距离、时间等。可用作形式主语、形式宾语或用在强调句型中。

It's me. Open the door, please.
是我，请开门。
It is cold.
天气冷。
It's about ten kilometers from the park to the museum.
公园到博物馆大约是十千米。
What time is it now? It's half past nine.
现在几点了？九点半。
It's very important for us to learn English well.
（实际主语是 to learn English well）
对我们来说，学好英语很重要。
I found it hard to fly a kite. （实际主语是 to fly a kite）
"they"有时代替一般人。
They say you are good at computer.
他们说你精通计算机。

三、物主代词

表示所有关系的代词叫作物主代词。物主代词可分为形容词性物主代词和名词性物主代词两种，见表2：

表2　物主代词

项目	我的	你的	他的	她的	它的	我们的	你们的	他们的
形容词性物主代词	my	your	his	her	its	our	your	their
名词性物主代词	mine	yours		hers		ours	yours	theirs

形容词性物主代词可用作定语，例如：
I love my country.
我热爱我的国家。
Is this your car?
这是你的汽车吗？
名词性物主代词可用作主语、宾语、表语以及与"of"连接的定语。
That car is mine, not yours.
那辆汽车是我的，不是你的。
These books are ours.
这些书是我们的。
Whose bag is it? It's hers.
这是谁的书包？是她的。

Yesterday I met a friend of mine in the street.
昨天我在街上碰见了我的一位朋友。

四、反身代词

反身代词表示我自己，你自己，他自己，我们自己，你们自己，他们自己等，指主语与宾语为同一人或物，或表示一个动作回到该动作执行者身上时，要用反身代词（否则就不能用反身代词），反身代词也可以放在名词或代词（主格）后面（也可以放在句尾）起强调作用。

反身代词第一、第二人称是由形容词性物主代词加"-self"（复数加-selves）构成的。第三人称反身代词是由人称代词宾格形式加-self（复数加-selves）构成的。具体内容见表3。

表3 反身代词

项目	第一人称	第二人称	第三人称		
单数	myself	yourself	himself	herself	itself
复数	ourselves	yourselves	themselves		

反身代词可用作宾语、主语的同位语和宾语的同位语。用作同位语时表示强调"本人、自己"。

I am teaching myself computer.
我自学计算机。
Take good care of yourself.
把自己照顾好。
The child himself drew this picture.
孩子自己画的这张画。
You should ask the children themselves.
你应该问一问孩子们自己。

五、相互代词

表示相互关系的代词叫相互代词，它们表示句中动词所叙述的动作或感觉在涉及的各个对象之间是相互存在的，有each other 和one another 两组，但在运用中，这两组词没什么区别。

如：They love each other.
他们彼此相爱。
It is easy to see that the people of different cultures have always copied each other.
显而易见，不同文化的人总是相互借鉴的。
He put all the books beside one another.
他把所有书并列摆放起来。
Usually these small groups were independent of each other.
这些小团体通常是相互独立的。

The students borrowed each other's notes.

学生们互借笔记。

六、指示代词

表示这个、那个、这些、那些以及 it, such, same 等的词叫作指示代词。指示代词在句中作主语、宾语、表语、定语。

What do you like? I like this.

你喜欢什么？我喜欢这个。

That is a red car.

那是一辆红色汽车。

I should say I know that.

我应该说我知道这件事情。

注意：this 和 these 表示在时间上或空间上较近的人或物。that 和 those 表示在时间上或空间上较远的人或物。

This is a book. 这是一本书。

These are cars. 这些是汽车。

I am busy these days. 我这些日子很忙。

That is not a room. 那不是一间房间。

Those are trees. 那些是树。

指示代词分单数（this/that）和复数（these/those）两种形式，既可作限定词又可作代词，例如：

限定词：This girl is Mary. Those men are my teachers.

代词：This is Mary. Those are my teachers.

七、疑问代词

表示"谁（who），谁（whom），谁的（whose），什么（what），哪个或哪些（which）"等的词叫疑问代词。

疑问代词都可用作连接代词或引导名词性从句（主语从句、宾语从句、表语从句和同位语从句）。

Tell me who he is.

告诉我他是谁。

What we should do is still unknown.

我们该干什么仍然还不知道。

I know whom he is looking for.

我知道他在找谁。

疑问代词用于特殊疑问句中时一般放在句子的最前面，在句中可用作主语、宾语、表语、定语。

Who is here just now?

刚才谁在这儿？

Whom are you looking for?
你在找谁?
Whose exercise-book is this?
这是谁的练习本?
What is this?
这是什么?
Which one do you like, this one or that one?
你喜欢哪一个,这个还是那个?

八、关系代词

关系代词是用来引导定语从句的代词。关系代词有 who, whose, whom, that, which, as, 可用作引导从句的关联词,它们在句中可用作主语、表语、宾语、定语。在句中,它们还代表着从句所修饰的那个名词或代词(通称为先行词)。

This is the man who helped me yesterday.
这个男人昨天帮了我。
He said he saw me there, which was a lie.
他说在那儿看到了我,纯属谎言。
说明:关系代词 that 在从句中作宾语或表语时可省略,例如:
I've forgotten much of the Latin I once knew.
我过去懂拉丁语,现在大都忘了。

九、不定代词

没有明确指定代替任何特定名词或形容词的词叫作不定代词,常见的不定代词有 all, both, each, every 等,以及含 some-, any-, no-等的合成代词,如 something, anybody, no one。这些不定代词大都可以代替名词和形容词,在句中作主语、宾语、表语和定语。如:
—Do you have a car? —你有一辆小汽车吗?
—Yes, I have one. —是的,我有一辆。
—I don' know any of them. —他们,我一个也不认识。
any:一些,任何。any 多用在否定或疑问句中,在句中作主语、宾语、定语。any 作定语时,所修饰的名词没有单复数限制,一般多用复数,any 用在肯定句中,表示"任何"。
Do you have any books?
你有书吗?
You can come any time.
你什么时候都可以来。
some:一些,某些,某个。some 多用在肯定句中。表示邀请或者对方可能给予肯定回答时,可用在疑问句中。
There are a lot of flowers in the garden, some are white, which I like very much.
花园里有许多花,一些是白色的,我特别喜欢。
I am going to get some ink.

我去弄点墨水。
Will you have some coffee, please?
喝点咖啡吗?
no: 无,在句中作定语,表示否定,语气要比 not any 强。
She knows no English.
她根本就不懂英语。
I have no bike.
我没有自行车。
None 既可以指人也可以指物,其后通常接 of 短语,用作主语时,若指不可数名词,谓语只能用单数,若指复数名词时,则谓语可用单数(较正式),也可以用复数(非正式语体)。
None of the milk can be used.
这些牛奶都不能用了。
None of the films is/are worth seeing.
这些电影没有一部值得一看。
many: 许多,在句中作主语、宾语、定语。many 在句中代替可数名词。
I have many books to give you.
我有许多书要给你。
Many of the students like English very much.
许多学生非常喜欢英语。
much: 许多。在句中作主语、宾语、定语。much 在句中代替不可数名词。
There is not much ink in the bottle.
瓶子里没多少墨水了。
a few, a little, few, little: 几个,一点儿,没几个,没多少。它们在句中作主语、宾语、定语,其中 a few 和 few 跟可数名词,a little 和 little 跟不可数名词,它们表示少量、不多、几个,只是主观上的一种相对说法,并没有具体的数量标准。
Few of the books are cheap now.
现在没几本书是便宜的。
A few friends came to see me yesterday.
昨天有几个朋友来看我。
I have a little money to buy the book.
我的这点钱能买这本书。
There is little water in the thermos.
暖水瓶没多少水了。

十、连接代词

连接代词主要包括 who, whom, what, which, whose, whoever, whatever, whichever, whomever 等,它们在句中可用作主语、宾语、表语、定语等,可以引导主语从句、宾语从句和表语从句,如:

I don't know who he is.
我不知道他是谁。
What he says sounds reasonable.
他说的话听起来有道理。
The question is who（m）we should trust.
问题是我们该信任谁。
I'll take whoever wants to go.
谁想去我就带谁去。
Take whichever seat you like.
你喜欢坐哪个座位就坐哪个。
I will just say whatever comes into my mind.
我想到什么就说什么。

真题分析

1. Our Chinese teacher likes to play football with _____ after school.
   A. we　　　　　B. our　　　　　C. us　　　　　D. ours
   分析：我们的语文老师放学后喜欢和我们一起踢足球。A 我们，人称代词主格；B 我们的，形容词性物主代词；C 我们，人称代词宾格；D 我们的，名词性物主代词。play football with sb.，与某人一起踢足球；当 sb. 是人称代词时，要用宾格形式，故选 C。

2. Shanghai is a little larger than _____ city in Japan.
   A. another　　　B. other　　　　C. any　　　　　D. any other
   分析：上海比日本的任何城市都稍大一些。another 用于泛指三个以上的不定数目中的"另一个"，后面可接单数名词，也可省略后面的名词，用作代词；other 别的/其他的，修饰单、复数名词；根据句意，A 和 B 两项不合语境，可排除。any 任何的，用在肯定句中修饰单数名词或不可数名词；any other 任何其他的。than any…表示"比所有……都……"，不排除被比较者（或主语）本身；than any other…表示"比所有其他的都……"，排除了被比较者（或主语）本身。根据实际情况，上海并不是日本的城市，可以和日本的任何一个城市相比，需用 any，故选 C。

3. —I'm sorry I made some mistakes in my exam.
   —It doesn't matter. _____ makes mistakes.
   A. Somebody　　B. None　　　　C. Everybody　　D. Nobody
   分析：——对不起，我在考试中犯了一些错。——没关系。每个人都会出错。Somebody 某人，none 没有人，everybody 每个人，nobody 没有人。根据 It doesn't matter 可知，对于考试犯错是没有关系的，因此表示每个人都会出错，故选 C。

4. —What kind of books do you like?
   —I like the books _____ are about successful people.
   A. that　　　　B. who　　　　C. whom　　　　D. whose
   分析：——你喜欢什么样的书？——我喜欢那些关于成功人士的书。A：that 没有词义，关系代词，作主语或宾语；B：who 谁，作主语或宾语；C：whom 谁，宾格，用在介词之后；D：whose 谁的，作定语；由句子结构可知，是定语从句，先行词 books 指物，在从句中作主语，要用关系代词 that。故选 A。

5. We just hope that Tom will bring _____ good news back home this time.
   A. a few   B. some   C. many   D. little

   分析：我们只希望汤姆这次能带些好消息回家。A 一些，其后跟可数名词复数；B 一些，后跟可数名词复数或不可数；C 一些，很多，后跟可数名词复数；D 几乎没有，其后跟不可数名词。根据题干中的 hope，可知此句表示肯定意义，且 news 是不可数名词，故选 B。

实战演练

( ) 1. Jim asked _____ to help him.
   A. I   B. me   C. he   D. she

( ) 2. May I have _____ coffee, please?
   A. some   B. any   C. the   D. a lot

( ) 3. His name is James, but he usually calls _____ Jim.
   A. he   B. him   C. his   D. himself

( ) 4. I hate the dogs _____ live in the next house. They make loud noises all night.
   A. who   B. that   C. what   D. whom

( ) 5. Tom, please pass _____ the glasses. I want to read the newspapers.
   A. you   B. me   C. my   D. your

( ) 6. Would you like _____ to drink?
   A. something   B. anything   C. nothing   D. everything

( ) 7. This isn't my T-shirt. _____ is blue.
   A. I   B. Me   C. Mine   D. My

( ) 8. —Where's your sister?
       —I don't know. Is _____ in the bedroom?
   A. he   B. she   C. him   D. her

( ) 9. —Who lives together with this old woman?
       —_____. She lives alone.
   A. Nobody   B. Somebody   C. Anybody   D. Everybody

( ) 10. —Dad, can you help me? There is _____ wrong with my computer.
        —OK, I'm coming.
   A. nothing   B. everything   C. anything   D. something

( ) 11. Mr. Wang likes cleaning _____ room.
   A. his   B. hers   C. him   D. it

( ) 12. Look! An old man is crossing the road. Let's go and help _____.
   A. he   B. him   C. she   D. her

( ) 13. _____ Anna's parents are teachers and they work in the same school.
   A. Some   B. Any   C. Both   D. All

( ) 14. Dave's father gave him _____ money for the school trip.
　　A. few　　　B. many　　　　C. some　　　　D. any

( ) 15. _____ did you slow down? We are already late for the meeting.
　　A. How　　　B. When　　　　C. Why　　　　D. Where

( ) 16. The bananas are on the shelf. _____ are very nice.
　　A. They　　　B. You　　　　C. We　　　　D. Theirs

( ) 17. —Who's that tall boy?
　　—_____ name is Tom.
　　A. His　　　B. Her　　　　C. Your　　　　D. My

( ) 18. —Jim and Sonia, have you brought your paintings?
　　—Yes, we have. Look, these are _____.
　　A. we　　　B. ours　　　　C. us　　　　D. our

( ) 19. Larry, please pass _____ the dictionary.
　　A. I　　　B. me　　　　C. my　　　　D. mine

( ) 20. The computer works well. There is _____ wrong with it.
　　A. something　　　　　　B. anything
　　C. nothing　　　　　　　D. everything

( ) 21. British people usually shake hands the first time _____ meet.
　　A. they　　　B. you　　　　C. we　　　　D. I

( ) 22. —Is this your key, Jenny?
　　—No, _____ is in my handbag.
　　A. His　　　B. Hers　　　　C. Mine　　　　D. Yours

( ) 23. —Who helped Jessie with her English?
　　—_____, she taught herself.
　　A. Anybody　　B. Somebody　　C. Nobody　　D. Everybody

( ) 24. Miss Yang teaches _____ English. She is _____ favorite teacher.
　　A. us; ours　　B. we; ours　　C. our; us　　D. us; our

( ) 25. Helen asked _____ to help her.
　　A. I　　　B. me　　　　C. he　　　　D. she

( ) 26. At last, he reached a lonely island _____ was completely cut off from the outside world.
　　A. when　　　B. which　　　C. where　　　D. whom

( ) 27. My brother and I like basketball. _____ play it together once a week.
　　A. I　　　B. They　　　　C. We　　　　D. You

( ) 28. Does he live in the house _____ windows face south?
　　A. that　　　B. which　　　C. whose　　　D. where

( ) 29. —Is this Kate's bicycle?
　　—No, _____ is under the tree. She put it there this morning.
　　A. his　　　B. hers　　　　C. mine　　　　D. yours

( ) 30. —Have you found the information about famous people _____ you can use for the report?
—Not yet. I'll search some on the Internet.
A. which B. who C. what D. whom

第四节　形容词

一、形容词的定义

表示人或事物的属性、特征或状态的词叫形容词（adjective 简称 adj.）。形容词修饰名词；它的基本用法就是为名词提供更多的信息，一般放在所修饰的名词之前；若修饰不定代词，则需后置。以-y，-able，-al，-ful，-ic，-ish，-less，-ous 等后缀结尾的词，一般是形容词，如：rainy（多雨的），changeable（多变的），medical（医学上的），careful（仔细的），atomic（原子的），foolish（愚蠢的），careless（粗心的），delicious（美味的），healthy（健康的）等。

二、形容词的用法

1. 用作定语。

Li Mei is a beautiful city girl.

李梅是一个漂亮的城市女孩。

The new student comes from Japan.

那个新学生来自日本。

2. 用作表语。

My father's car is very expensive.

我父亲的轿车很贵。

The English story is very interesting.

那个英文故事很有趣。

3. 用作宾语补足语。

Don't keep the door open.

别让门一直开着。

His success made him happy.

他的成功让他感到幸福。

We finally found the dictionary very useful.

我们最后发现词典很有用。

4. 用作状语或补语。

These soldiers spent three days in the cold weather, cold and hungry.

士兵们又冷又饿地在严寒的气候中度过了三天。

After seven days, the children came back from the forest safe.

七天之后，孩子们安全地从森林中返回。

5. 少数形容词只能作表语，不能作定语。

这些形容词包括 ill, asleep, awake, alone, alive, well, worth, glad, unable, afraid 等。

（正）Don't be afraid.

（误）Mr. Li is an afraid man.

（正）The old man was ill yesterday.

（误）This is an ill person.

（正）This place is worth visiting.

（误）That is a worth book.

6. 少数形容词只能作定语，不能作表语。

这些形容词包括 little, live（活着的）, elder, eldest 等。

（正）My elder brother is a doctor.

（误）My brother is elder than l.

（正）This is a little house.

（误）The house is little.

（正）Do you want live fish or dead one?

（误）The old monkey is still live.

7. "the + 形容词" 表示一类人或事物，相当于名词，用作主语及宾语。

The old often think of old things.

老年人经常回想往事。

The new always take the place of the old.

新事物总会取代旧事物。

三、形容词的位置

单个形容词修饰名词时，一般要放在名词的前面。它们的前面常常带有冠词、形容词性物主代词、指示代词、数词等。

a red flower 一朵红花

this interesting story 这个有趣的故事

six blind men 六个盲人

my own house 我自己的房子

1. 当形容词所修饰的词是由 some, any, every, no 等构成的不定代词时，形容词必须置于所修饰的词之后。

She has something new to tell me.

她有一些新的情况要告诉我。

l have nothing important to do today.

今天我没有重要的事要做。

Do you know anybody else here?

这儿你还有认识的人吗？

2. 形容词后面有介词短语或不定式短语时，形容词必须置于名词之后。

lt is a problem difficult to work out.

这是一个难以解决的问题。

Edison is a student difficult to teach.

爱迪生是个难教的学生。

This is a kind of flowers easy to grow.

这是一种易栽的花。

3. 在以下特殊用法中,形容词置于所修饰的名词之后。

All people, young or old, should be strict with themselves.

所有的人,无论老少,都应该严格要求自己。

We are building a new school, modern and super.

我们正在建一所现代化的高档次的新型学校。

All countries, rich and poor, should help one another.

所有的国家,无论穷富,都应该互相帮助。

4. 有少数形容词,如 enough 和 possible,既可置于所修饰的名词之前,也可置于所修饰的名词之后。例如:

Do you have enough time (time enough) to prepare?

你有足够的时间做准备吗?

Maybe it will be a possible chance (chance possible) for you.

或许它将成为你的一次可能的机遇。

5. 有些形容词,置于名词之前与之后,含义不尽相同。

the writer present 出席的作家

the present writer 当代的作家

四、形容词的比较级和最高级

(一) 形容词的比较级和最高级的构成规则

1. 一般单音节词和少数以-er,-ow 结尾的双音节词,比较级在后面加-er,最高级在后面加-est。

(1) 单音节词。

small→smaller→smallest

short→shorter→shortest

tall→taller→tallest

great→greater→greatest

(2) 双音节词。

clever→cleverer→cleverest

narrow→narrower→narrowest

2. 以不发音字母 e 结尾的单音节词,比较级在原级后加-r,最高级在原级后加-st。

large→larger→largest

nice→nicer→nicest

3. 在重读闭音节(即:辅音字母 + 元音字母 + 辅音字母)中,先双写末尾的辅音字母,比较级加-er,最高级加-est。

big→bigger→biggest
hot→hotter→hottest
fat→fatter→fattest

4. 以"辅音字母＋y"结尾的双音节词，把 y 改为 i，比较级加-er，最高级加-est。

easy→easier→easiest
heavy→heavier→heaviest
busy→busier→busiest
happy→happier→happiest

5. 其他双音节词和多音节词，比较级在前面加 more，最高级在前面加 most。

beautiful→more beautiful→most beautiful
different→more different→most different
easily→more easily→most easily

注意：
（1）形容词最高级前通常必须用定冠词 the，副词最高级前可不用。
The Sahara is the biggest desert in the world.
（2）形容词 most 前面没有 the，不表示最高级的含义，只表示"非常"。
It is a most important problem.
＝It is a very important problem.

6. 有少数形容词、副词的比较级和最高级是不规则的，必须熟记。

good→better→best   well→better→best
bad→worse→worst   ill→worse→worst
old→older/elder→oldest/eldest
many/much→more→most   little→less→least
far →further/farther→ furthest/farthest

（二）形容词、副词的比较级和最高级的用法

1. "A＋be＋形容词比较级＋than＋B"意思为"A 比 B 更……"。
如：This tree is taller than that one. 这棵树比那棵树高。
注意：
①在含有连词 than 的比较级中，前后的比较对象必须是同一范畴，即同类事物之间的比较。
②在比较级前面使用 much，表示程度"强得多"。
如：A watermelon is much bigger than an apple.
③very，quite 一般只能修饰原级，不能修饰比较级。

2. "比较级＋and＋比较级"表示"越来越……"。
It becomes warmer and warmer when spring comes.
春天来了，天气变得越来越暖和了。
It is getting cooler and cooler.
天气越来越凉爽。
The wind became more and more heavily.
风变得越来越大。

Our school is becoming more and more beautiful.

我们的学校变得越来越美丽。

3. 在含有 or 的选择疑问句中，如果有两者供选择，前面的形容词要用比较级形式。

Who is taller, Tim or Tom? 谁更高，Tim 还是 Tom?

4. "the + 比较级……，the + 比较级……"，表示"越……越……"。

The more money you make, the more you spend.

钱你赚得越多，花得越多。

The sooner, the better.

越快越好。

5. 表示倍数的比较级用法。

（1） A is…times the size /height/length/width of B.

The new building is three times the height of the old one.

新楼是旧楼的三倍高。

（2） A is…times as big /high/long/wide/large as B.

Asia is four times as large as Europe.

亚洲是欧洲的四倍大。

（3） A is…times larger /higher/longer/wider than B.

Our school is twice bigger than yours.

我们学校比你们学校大两倍。

6. 形容词、副词的最高级形式主要用来表示三者或三者以上人或事物的比较，表示"最……"的意思。句子中有表示范围的词或短语。如：of the three, in our class 等。

He is the tallest in our class.

他在我们班里是最高的。

7. 比较级与最高级的转换。

Mike is the most intelligent in his class.

Mike is more intelligent than any other student in his class.

8. 可修饰比较级的词和短语有 rather, much, far, any, still, even, many, by far, a bit, a little, a lot, a great deal 等。

He is much taller than me.

他比我高得多。

It runs even faster than a deer.

它跑得甚至比鹿还要快。

9. 可修饰最高级的词有 much, nearly, almost 等。

This hat is nearly/almost the biggest.

注意：

a. very 可修饰最高级，但位置与 much 不同。

This is the very best.

This is much the best.

b. 序数词通常只修饰最高级。

Africa is the second largest continent.

10. 要避免重复使用比较级。

（错）He is more cleverer than his brother.

（对）He is more clever than his brother.

（对）He is cleverer than his brother.

11. 要注意对应句型，遵循前后一致的原则。

The population of Shanghai is larger than that of Beijing.

上海的人口比北京的人口多。

It is easier to make a plan than to carry it out.

制订计划比执行计划容易。

12. 要注意冠词的使用，后有名词的时候，前面才有可能有冠词。

Which is larger, Canada or Australia?

Which is the larger country, Canada or Australia?

She is taller than her two sisters.

She is the taller of the two sisters.

真题分析

1. Just be _____, you can't lose your weight in a day.
   A. careful B. patient C. honest D. brave

   分析：要有耐心，你不可能在一天中减肥。A. 小心的，仔细的；B. 有耐心的；C. 诚实的；D. 勇敢的。根据常识可知，不可能一天就能有减肥成效，要有耐心，故答案选 B。

2. —Who will you ask to help with the work, Lucy or Lily?
   —Lily. She is much _____.
   A. careful B. more careful C. most careful D. carefully

   分析：—你将让谁帮助你工作，露西还是丽丽？—丽丽，她更细心。much 修饰形容词的比较级形式，故答案选 B。

3. Linda is _____ of the three girls, but she is the tallest.
   A. young B. younger C. youngest D. the youngest

   分析：琳达是三个女孩中最小的，但她是最高的。young 年轻的，原级；younger 更年轻的，比较级；the youngest 最年轻的，最高级。根据 three girls 可知三者作比较，用最高级，形容词最高级前要加 the，故答案选 D。

4. The more you smile to others, the _____ you will feel.
   A. happier B. happy C. more happily D. more happier

   分析：你对别人微笑越多，你就感到越高兴。the + 比较级 + 句式，the + 比较级 + 句子，表示越……，越……，固定句式，happy 的比较级是 happier，故答案选 A。

5. Tina is as _____ as her sister, Tara.
   A. outgoing B. more outgoing
   C. the most outgoing D. the more outgoing

   分析：蒂娜和她姐姐塔拉一样外向。as...as 表示和……一样。中间用形容词原级，outgoing 外向的，原级；more outgoing，比较级；the most outgoing，最高级，故答案选 A。

实战演练

( ) 1. Meiwei Restaurant is _____ than Haoyun Restaurant.
　　A. near　　　B. nearer　　　C. nearest　　　D. the near

( ) 2. He jumps much _____ than I.
　　A. far　　　B. father　　　C. farther　　　D. farthest

( ) 3. —Do you know Shanghai is one of _____ in the world?
　　—Yes, it's bigger than _____ city in China.
　　A. the biggest city; any　　　B. the biggest cities; any
　　C. the biggest cities; any other　　　D. the biggest city; any other

( ) 4. Mr. Li asks us to remember that _____ careful we are, _____ mistakes we will make.
　　A. the fewer; the more　　　B. the more; the fewer
　　C. the more; the more　　　D. the fewer; the fewer

( ) 5. —If you don't like the red coat, take the blue one.
　　—OK, but do you have _____ size in blue? This one is a bit tight for me.
　　A. big　　　B. a bigger　　　C. the big　　　D. the bigger

( ) 6. It is already April, but it is still _____ in the north of China.
　　A. warm　　　B. cold　　　C. rainy　　　D. hot

( ) 7. Which is _____, the telephone, the computer or the light bulb?
　　A. useful　　　B. more useful　　　C. most useful　　　D. the most useful

( ) 8. Jeff exercises every day. He is the _____ in his class.
　　A. longer　　　B. longest　　　C. stronger　　　D. strongest

( ) 9. —Is that Tom? He is tall.
　　—Yes, Tom is the _____ in his class.
　　A. clever　　　B. taller　　　C. tallest　　　D. thin

( ) 10. —Let's buy some cards for our teachers.
　　—Why not make some ourselves? It will be much _____.
　　A. interesting　　　B. more interesting
　　C. most interesting　　　D. the most interesting

( ) 11. Although he's eaten up two bowls of rice, he still doesn't feel _____.
　　A. full enough　　　B. enough full
　　C. enough fully　　　D. fully enough

( ) 12. —How did you lose the soccer match?
　　—We had _____ players. They had eleven while we had only nine!
　　A. less　　　B. better　　　C. fewer　　　D. more

( ) 13. People live longer and stay _____ today than they did 50 years ago.
　　A. health　　　B. healthier　　　C. healthiest　　　D. the healthiest

( ) 14. Li Hua's shoes are _____ than Zhang Hui's.
　　　　A. cheap　　B. cheaper　　　　C. the cheaper　　　D. the cheapest

( ) 15. The Yangtze River（长江）is one of the _____ rivers in the world.
　　　　A. long　　B. longer　　　　C. longest　　　　D. most longest

( ) 16. Mr. Liu is really a nice person—the _____ person I know.
　　　　A. nicer　　B. nicest　　　　C. happier　　　　D. happiest

( ) 17. Lucy is _____ student because she was born later than anyone else in her class.
　　　　A. young　　B. younger　　　　C. the younger　　　D. the youngest

( ) 18. I'm sorry I'm late. I should get here 10 minutes _____.
　　　　A. early　　B. earlier　　　　C. the earlier　　　D. the earliest

( ) 19. Who is _____, Tom, Jack or Bill?
　　　　A. the most carefully　　　　　B. more carefully
　　　　C. the most careful　　　　　　D. more careful

( ) 20. Traveling abroad is much _____ than before.
　　　　A. easy　　B. easier　　　　C. easiest　　　　D. the easiest

第五节　副词

一、副词的定义

副词（adverb 简称 adv.）是指在句子中表示行为或状态特征的词，用以修饰动词、形容词、其他副词或全句，表示时间、地点、程度、方式等。

二、副词的分类

1. 时间频率副词。

时间频率副词主要表示"什么时候""经常与否"，表明动作所做的次数或频繁程度。如：now，then，often，always，usually，next，after，already（已经），generally（一般地），frequently（频繁），seldom/hardly（很少地），ever，never，yet，soon，too，immediately（立即），finally，shortly（很快），before，ago，sometimes，yesterday，once，twice，lately，recently，yet 等。

2. 地点副词。

地点副词是表示地点与位置关系的副词，用来说明动作是在什么地方发生的。如：here，there，everywhere，anywhere，somewhere，in，out，inside，outside，above，below，up，down，back，forward（向前的），home，upstairs，downstairs，across，along，round，around，near，off，past，up，away，on 等。

3. 方式副词。

方式副词表示行为动作发生的方式。如：carefully，properly（适当地），anxiously（焦虑地），suddenly，normally（正常地），fast，well，calmly（冷静地），politely（有礼貌地），proudly（自豪地），softly，warmly，slowly，badly，hard，bravely 等。

4. 程度副词。

程度副词是对一个形容词或者副词在程度上加以限定或修饰的副词。如：much, little, very, rather（相当），so, too, still, quite, perfectly（完美地），enough, extremely（非常），entirely（整个），almost, slightly（细小地），hardly 等。

5. 疑问副词。

疑问副词用来引导特殊疑问句，表示时间、地点、方式、原因等。如：how, when, where, why。

6. 关系副词。

关系副词用于引导定语从句，在从句中用作状语，表示时间、地点，以及原因。如：when, where, why。

7. 连接副词。

连接副词可分为两类，一类用于连接句子或从句，常见的有 therefore, besides, otherwise, however, moreover, still, thus, meanwhile 等；另一类用于引导从句或不定式，主要的有 when, why, where, how 等。

8. 表顺序的副词。

这些副词有 first, then, next, finally, afterwards, primarily 等。

9. 完成时的副词。

这些副词有 already, ever, just, never, since, yet, recently 等。

三、副词的用法

副词在句中可作状语、表语、补语、定语。

He works hard.（作状语）

他努力工作。

You speak English very well.（作状语）

你英语讲得相当好。

Does she stay home?（作表语）

她待在家吗？

she stays home 是主系表结构，stay 此处是系动词，home 是副词。

Let's be out.（作表语）

让我们出去吧。

Food here is hard to get.

(here 作状语，hard 作表语)

这儿很难弄到食物。

Let him out!（作补语）

让他出去！

四、副词在句中的位置

1. 多数副词放在动词后面，或者放在 be 动词、助动词或情态动词之后，实义动词之前。如果实义动词后有宾语，则放于宾语之后。

I can also do that.

我也可以这样做。

I also want to play that game.

我也想玩这游戏。

I get up early in the morning every day.

每一天的早晨我都起得很早。

He has eaten enough.

他已经吃饱了。

We can go to this school freely.

我们可以免费到这家学校学习。

I have seen this film twice with my friends.

这部电影我和朋友看过两次。

2. 副词修饰形容词时，一般放在被修饰词之前，但 enough 除外。

It's very easy, and I can do it.

这很容易，我能做到。

It's rather difficult to tell who is right.

很难说谁是对的。

He didn't run fast enough to catch the train.

他的奔跑速度不足以快到能够追上火车。

3. 频度副词可放在实义动词的前面，情态动词和助动词的后面。

I often help him these days.

这些日子我经常帮助他。

I always remember the day when I first came to this school.

我常常记得我第一次来学校的那一天。

You couldn't always help me.

你不能老是帮助我。

We usually go shopping once a week.

我们通常一周买一次东西。

The new students don't always go to dance.

新学生并不时常去跳舞。

4. 疑问副词、连接副词、关系副词以及修饰整个句子的副词，通常放在句子或从句的前面。

When do you study every day?

你每天什么时间学习？

Can you tell me how you did it?

你能告诉我你如何做的吗？

First, let me ask you some questions.

先让我来问你几个问题。

How much does this bicycle cost?

这辆自行车多少钱？

The students were reading when the teacher came into the classroom.

当老师进教室时，学生们正在读书。

5. 时间副词和地点副词在一个句子中，地点副词在前面，时间副词在后面。

We went shopping in the supermarket at 9 o'clock yesterday.

昨天九点钟我们到超市买东西了.

What were you doing in the classroom yesterday afternoon?

昨天下午你在教室里干什么？

The accident took place in the Eleven Avenue one hour ago.

这场事故在一小时前发生在十一号大街。

6. 否定副词在句首，句子要部分倒装。

Never have I felt so excited!

我从来没有觉得这么激动！

真题分析

1. I jumped _____ than Bill in the sports meet last year.
   A. high   B. higher   C. highest   D. the highest

   分析：去年我在运动会上比比尔跳得高。A. high 是原级；B. higher 是比较级；C. highest 是最高级；D. the highest 是最高级。最高级用于三者之间做比较，但是常常与定冠词 the 连用。than 比……，用于两者比较的句子中，所以该句用比较级，故选 B。

2. —What's the weather like in summer here?
   —It's hot. Sometimes it rains _____ .
   A. clearly   B. heavily   C. carefully   D. heavy

   分析：——夏天这里的天气怎么样？——它是炎热的。有时天下大雨。A. 清楚地；B. 程度严重地；C. 仔细地；D. 重的。rain heavily，下大雨，故选 B。

3. —_____ do you sleep every day, Eric?
   —For about eight hours.
   A. How much   B. How fast   C. How often   D. How long

   分析：——艾瑞克，你每天晚上睡多长时间？——大约八个小时。A. 多少；B. 多快；C. 多长时间一次；D. 多长。根据答语 For about eight hours，可知问句询问的是时间长短，对时间长短提问应使用 how long，故答案是 D。

4. I can _____ understand it because you speak very quickly.
   A. almost   B. probably   C. mostly   D. hardly

   分析：我几乎听不懂，因为你说得太快了。A. almost 几乎；B. probably 可能；C. mostly 主要地；D. hardly 几乎不。根据 because you speak very quickly 可知对方几乎没听懂，故选 D。

5. Apples are _____ good fruit that _____ people dislike them.
   A. such, few   B. so, few   C. such, a few   D. so, a few

   分析：苹果是那么好的水果以至于几乎没有人不喜欢他们。So 如此，那么，用法是 so +

形容词。such 如此，那么，用法是：such + (a/an) + (形容词) + 名词，但名词前有 few, little, many, much 修饰时只用 so，few 几乎没有，a few，几个。结合句意，故选 A。

实战演练

( ) 1. —Are you feeling _____?
　　—Yes, I'm fine now.
　　A. any well　　B. any better　　C. quite good　　D. quite better

( ) 2. The experiment was _____ easier than we had expected.
　　A. more　　B. much more　　C. much　　D. more much

( ) 3. If there were no examinations, we should have _____ at school.
　　A. the happiest time　　B. a more happier time
　　C. much happiest time　　D. a much happier time

( ) 4. —_____ is the ticket to Garden Expo?
　　—It's about 100 yuan.
　　A. How much　　B. How many
　　C. How long　　D. How often

( ) 5. —Please tell me _____.
　　—Next Saturday.
　　A. when did we have a party　　B. when will we have a party
　　C. when we had a party　　D. when we will have a party

( ) 6. —I hear Peter has gone to Sanya for his holiday.
　　—How nice! Do you know _____?
　　A. when he left　　B. when he was leaving
　　C. when did he leave　　D. when was he leaving

( ) 7. —_____ do you go to the gym?
　　—Once a week.
　　A. How much　　B. How often
　　C. How soon　　D. How long

( ) 8. —Which season do you like _____, spring or autumn?
　　—Spring, because everything is full of energy.
　　A. good　　B. better　　C. best　　D. well

( ) 9. We can hardly believe that you learn to dance so _____.
　　A. quick　　B. quickly　　C. useful　　D. usefully

( ) 10. Who listens _____, Tom, Jack or Bill?
　　A. the most carefully　　B. more carefully
　　C. the most careful　　D. more careful

( ) 11. —Could you tell me _____ the party is?
　　—In the school hall.
　　A. where　　B. when　　C. what　　D. how

( ) 12. —Jimmy, where are my glasses? I have looked everywhere.
　　　 —Oh, Granny. They are _____ on your nose.
　　　　　A. even　　　B. well　　　　　　C. right　　　　　　D. ever

( ) 13. I was so tired that I could _____ walk any farther.
　　　　　A. nearly　　B. hardly　　　　　C. really　　　　　 D. suddenly

( ) 14. In America when you're given a present, you can open it _____. You don't have to wait.
　　　　　A. immediately　　　　　　　　B. properly
　　　　　C. carefully　　　　　　　　　　D. quietly

( ) 15. I got up _____ today.
　　　　　A. later　　　B. more lately　　　C. lately　　　　　 D. late

( ) 16. In Britain tea _____ with milk or sugar in it.
　　　　　A. usually drinks　　　　　　　 B. is usually drunk
　　　　　C. usually is drunk　　　　　　 D. drank usually

( ) 17. He _____ to school to clean his classroom.
　　　　　A. always comes early　　　　　B. comes always early
　　　　　C. always early comes　　　　　D. come always earlier

( ) 18. She likes reading and _____.
　　　　　A. so I do　　B. I do so　　　　 C. I like so　　　　 D. so do I

( ) 19. That maths problem is _____ difficult _____ nobody can work it out.
　　　　　A. too; to　　　　　　　　　　　B. very; that
　　　　　C. so; that　　　　　　　　　　　D. very; but

( ) 20. I am so tired that I can't walk _____.
　　　　　A. much far　　　　　　　　　　B. any farther
　　　　　C. even far　　　　　　　　　　 D. very further

第六节　数词

一、数词的定义

数词（numeral 简称 num.）是指表示数目多少或顺序先后的词。英语中的数词分为基数词和序数词，基数词是表示数目多少的数词，如：1（one），2（two），3（three）…。序数词是表示次序、顺序的数词，如：第一（first），第二（second），第三（third）…。

二、基数词

基数词用来表示数目多少，它包括表示数字的所有单词。记忆这些单词可以用数字构成分类记忆法。

1. 基数词的构成。

1~12 的数字（表4）

个位数和 10，11，12 这些数字是一个单词独立的数词。

表 4 1~12 的数字

1 – one	2 – two	3 – three
4 – four	5 – five	6 – six
7 – seven	8 – eight	9 – nine
10 – ten	11 – eleven	12 – twelve

13~19 的数字（表 5）

13~19 的数字的单词由对应的个位数加后缀 teen 构成，但要注意 13，15，18 基数词构成。

表 5 13~19 的数字

13 – thirteen	14 – fourteen
15 – fifteen	16 – sixteen
17 – seventeen	18 – eighteen
19 – nineteen	

20~99 的数字（表 6）

20~90 的整十位数——由 2~9 加后缀 ty 构成，注意 20，30，40，50，80 的构成。

21~99 的非整数由"整十位数加个位数"构成，十位数与个位数之间用连字符"－"连接。

表 6 20~99 的数字（部分）

20 – twenty	22 – twenty-two
30 – thirty	33 – thirty-three
40 – forty	44 – forty-four
50 – fifty	55 – fifty-five
60 – sixty	67 – sixty-seven
70 – seventy	71 – seventy-one
80 – eighty	88 – eighty-eight
90 – ninety	96 – ninety-six

100~999 的数字（表 7）

100~900 的整百位数由 1~9 后面加 hundred（百）构成。

101~999 的非整百位数由"整百位数 and 整十位数－个位数"构成。如果没有整十位数或个位数则没有"-"。

表7 100~999 的数字（部分）

100 a/one hundred	101 one hundred and one
200 two hundred	232 two hundred and thirty-two
300 three hundred	320 three hundred and twenty
400 four hundred	444 four hundred and forty-four
500 five hundred	507 five hundred and seven
600 six hundred	621 six hundred and twenty-one
700 seven hundred	796 seven hundred and ninety-six
800 eight hundred	811 eight hundred and eleven
900 nine hundred	999 nine hundred and ninety-nine

千以上的数字（表8）

英语中没有专门表示"万""亿"的词，但有表示"千（thousand）"，"百万（million）"，"十亿（billion）"的词。英语把数字从右向左每三位分为一组，如"1000000000"对其进行分组成"1,000,000,000"，在这个数字中从右向左数第4位是千，第7位是百万，第十位是十亿。

表8 千以上的数字

一千 a/one thousand	五千 five thousand
一万 ten thousand	六万 sixty thousand
十万 a/one hundred thousand	九十万 nine hundred thousand
一百万 a/one million	四百万 four million
一千万 ten million	七千万 seventy million
一亿 one hundred million	三亿 three hundred million
十亿 a/one billion	二十亿 two billion

2. 基数词的用法。

（1）表示时刻。

在英语中时刻是用基数词来表示的，最常见的形式有三种：

a. 先点钟后分钟。如：6：30 six thirty， 7：52 seven fifty-two

b. 先分钟后点钟。表示"分钟数不超半小时"用"分钟数＋past＋点钟数"表示，如：
5：25   twenty-five past five

表示"分钟数超过半小时"用"（60－分钟数）＋to＋下一个点钟数"表示，如：
10：43   seventeen to eleven

c. 表示"整点"，直接用"点钟数（＋o'clock）"表示。"半点钟"用half表示，"一刻钟"用a quarter表示。如：

6：00 six（o'clock）   10：30 half past ten
4：45 a quarter to five   7：15 a quarter past seven

（2）表示年龄。
在英语中年龄用"岁数基数词＋year（s）old（可以省略）"表示。如：
He is ten years old. ＝He is ten.
他十岁了。

（3）表示顺序、编号。
一般置于名词后。如：Unit 2（第二单元），Page 20（第二十页），如果数词前有No.，则"No.＋基数词"置于名词前。如：
Who's that in Picture 1?
图1中的人是谁？
He is a student in No. 9 Middle School.
他是第九中学的一名学生。

注意：
（1）表示住所时不用"No."。如：202房间 Room 202（读作 Room two o two）。
（2）电话号码用基数词，可单个读，重复的数字可用double。如：3866988 读作 three eight six six（double six）nine eight eight（double eight）。
（3）用于计算。
What's one plus two? 一加二等于多少？
It's three. 等于三。
（4）表示倍（次）数。两倍以上用"基数词＋times"表示。如：
once 一倍（次），twice 两倍（次），three times 三倍（次），five times 五倍（次）

3. 基数词的复数用法。
（1）当hundred（百），thousand（千），million（百万），billion（十亿）等数词用于表示不确定的数目且后接of短语时用复数。如：
Hundreds of them were killed in the earthquake.
在地震中，他们中有几百人死亡。
She has got thousands of pairs of shoes.
她有数千双鞋子。
Millions of trees are planted every year.
每年都要栽数百万棵树。
上述用法中，数词复数前一般不得与具体的数字连用。如不能说three millions of trees，只能说three million trees，但短语hundreds of, thousands of, millions of 等前面可以和表示不

确定数量的修饰语连用,如可以说:many/some/a few hundreds of students 等。

(2) 基数词的复数用于人,用"in one's—"结构表示人的年龄"几十岁"。如:

In his thirties, he became an officer.

在他三十多岁时,他成了一名军官。

She is in her early (late) twenties.

她现在二十一二(八九)岁了。

(3) 基数词的复数用于时间,用"in the-"结构表示"几十年代"时。如:

In the 1990s, Hong Kong and Macao returned to China.

在二十世纪九十年代,香港和澳门回归了祖国。

This story happened in the sixties.

这个故事发生在六十年代。

(4) 基数词的复数用于表示某个基数词的多个,如:

Two twos are four. 二二得四。

Four threes are twelve. 四乘三等于十二。

三、序数词

序数词用来表示次序,在汉语中表示为"第几",如:第一(first)、第二(second)、第三(third)……。序数词在书写时可以将 first 缩写为 1st, second 缩写为 2nd, third 缩写为 3rd。序数词除了第一、第二、第三或个位数为一、二、三结尾的序数词外,其他序数词都是以-th 结尾的,缩写也是对应的数字加-th,如 fourth(第四)缩写为 4th。

1. 序数词的构成。

(1) 第一、第二、第三的序数词(表9)。

表9 第一、第二、第三的序数词

中文	英文	英文缩写
第一	first	1st
第二	second	2nd
第三	third	3rd

It's a movie about the Second World War.

这是一部关于第二次世界大战的电影。

Andy is on the third seat.

安迪坐在第三个座位上。

He won the first prize.

他获得了第一名。

(2) 第四至第十九的序数词(表10)。

由对应的基数词加后缀-th 构成,要注意第五、第八、第九、第十二的拼写变化。

表 10　第四至第十九的序数词

第四	fourth（4th）	第十二	twelfth（12th）
第五	fifth（5th）	第十三	thirteenth（13th）
第六	sixth（6th）	第十四	fourteenth（14th）
第七	seventh（7th）	第十五	fifteenth（15th）
第八	eighth（8th）	第十六	sixteenth（16th）
第九	ninth（9th）	第十七	seventeenth（17th）
第十	tenth（10th）	第十八	eighteenth（18th）
第十一	eleventh（11th）	第十九	nineteenth（19th）

（3）第二十到第九十九的序数词（表11）。

20～90 整十位数序数词：将对应的基数词词尾中的 y 变为 i，然后加 eth 构成。

21～99 非整十位数序数词：十位数用基数词，个位数用相应的序数词。十位数和个位数之间用连字符"-"连接。

表 11　第二十到第九十九的序数词（部分）

第二十	twentieth（20th）	第二十一	twenty-first（21st）
第三十	thirtieth（30th）	第三十二	thirty-second（32nd）
第四十	fortieth（40th）	第四十三	forty-third（43rd）
第五十	fiftieth（50th）	第五十四	fifty-fourth（54th）
第六十	sixtieth（60th）	第六十五	sixty-fifth（65th）
第七十	seventieth（70th）	第七十六	seventy-sixth（76th）
第八十	eightieth（80th）	第八十七	eighty-seventh（87th）
第九十	ninetieth（90th）	第九十九	ninety-ninth（99th）

例句：

The twentieth day of this month is my ninth birthday.

这个月的第二十天是我九岁的生日。

The thirty-second President of the United States is Frankin D. Roosevelt.

美国第三十二任总统是富兰克林·罗斯福。

（4）百位以上的序数词。

将基数词的结尾部分变为序数词即可。

第一百 one hundredth（100th）

第二百零四 two hundred and fourth（204th）

第五百六十二 five hundred and sixty-second（562nd）

He is the three hundred and forty-sixth volunteer.

他是第三百四十六个志愿者。

I have one hundred sheep. The one hundredth sheep is black.

我有一百只绵羊，第一百只绵羊是黑色的。

2. 序数词的用法。

序数词在使用时，通常前面要加定冠词 the，其可以用来表示顺序、楼层、编号、日期中的日等。

（1）表示顺序，如：

I am always the first to come to school.

我总是第一个来学校的。

（2）表示楼层，如：

My aunt lives on the fourth floor.

我姑妈住在四楼。

（3）表示编号，其结构为：the＋序数词＋名词＝名词（首字母要大写）＋基数词。如：

第九部分 the ninth part = Part nine

第四课 the fourth lesson = Lesson Four

第六段 the sixth paragraph = Paragraph six

（4）用来表示年、月、日："年"用基数词，"日"用序数词，如：

1949 年 10 月 1 日——写法：October 1st, 1949 读作：October（the）first, nineteen forty-nine

2017 年 2 月 28 日——写法：February 28th, 2017 读作：February,（the）twenty-eighth, two thousand and seventeen

（5）用来表示分数词："分子"用基数词，"分母"用序数词，"分子"大于 1，序数词用复数形式。如：

1/5→one fifth；2/3→two thirds；4/7→four sevenths；1/2→a half；1/4→one fourth = a quarter；3/4→three fourths = three quarters；50%→fifty hundredths（fifty percent）

（6）序数词前冠词的使用。

a. 序数词前一般要用 the，但表示"又一，再一"的概念时，序数词前也可以用 a/an，如：

I'm in the third grade.

我上三年级。

The girl plans to buy a second piano.

那女孩打算买第二架钢琴。

You've done it three times. Why not try a fourth time？

你已经做了三次了，为什么不试第四次呢？

b. 序数词前可用物主代词，表示"……的第几个……"，如：

This is her twenty-third birthday.

这是她的第二十三个生日。

c. 序数词与名词构成复合形容词时，冠词的选用由名词而定。如：

There is a second-hand bookstore.

有一家二手书店。

真题分析

1. There were about six _____ students in the school building during the earthquake.
   A. hundred B. hundreds C. hundreds of D. hundred of

   分析：地震期间，校舍里大约有六百名学生。hundred，百，基数词，表示具体的数量，其前要用基数词；hundreds of + 可数名词复数，表示不确定的数量，固定短语。空格前有基数词 six，要用 hundred，故答案选 A。

2. When Huawei P20 came out, _____ people couldn't wait to buy one in our town.
   A. thousand B. thousands C. thousand of D. thousands of

   分析：当华为 P20 上市时，成千上万的人迫不及待地想在我们镇上买一台。thousand，千，其前有具体数词修饰时，用其单数形式，当其前没有具体数词修饰时，用其复数形式，且和 of 连用，thousands of，成千上万，这里没有具体数词修饰，故选 D。

3. The number of the students in our school is about four _____. _____ of them are girls.
   A. thousand；Two thirds   B. thousands；Two third
   C. thousands；Two thirds D. thousand；Two third

   分析：我们学校的学生人数大约是 4000 人。2/3 是女孩。four 基数词后用 thousand 的原形，分数表达形式是分子是基数词，分母是序数词，分子大于1，分母用复数形式，故 2/3 是 two thirds，故选 A。

4. There are _____ months in a year. My birthday is in the _____ month.
   A. twelve；twelve   B. twelfth；twelfth
   C. twelve；twelfth   D. twelfth；twelve

   分析：一年有 12 个月，我的生日在第 12 个月。名词复数 months 前是基数词，twelve 是基数词，the 定冠词后是序数词，twelfth 是序数词，故选 C。

5. Ma Yun has decided to retire from his company in his _____.
   A. fifty B. fifties C. fiftieth D. fiftieths

   分析：马云已经决定在他 50 多岁时从他的公司退休。in one's + 基数词复数，表示在某人几十多岁时，in one's fifties，在某人五十多岁时，故选 B。

实战演练

( ) 1. _____ tourists come to visit the Great Wall during the vacation.
   A. Thousand   B. Thousand of
   C. Thousands of D. Thousands

( ) 2. —How many American students came to visit your school yesterday?
   —Nine. Five are from New York, and the other _____ are from Boston.
   A. two B. three C. four D. five

( ) 3. —What is five and six? Do you know?
   —Yes, it's _____.
   A. nine B. eleven C. thirteen D. fifteen

(　　) 4. There are _____ floors in the building and my home is on the _____ floor.
　　　A. eleven; seventh　　　　　　　B. eleven; seven
　　　C. eleventh; seven　　　　　　　D. eleventh; seventh

(　　) 5. _____ people come to Jilin to visit Mount Changbai every day.
　　　A. Thousands of　　　　　　　　B. Thousand of
　　　C. Thousands　　　　　　　　　D. Thousand

(　　) 6. Nine _____ pounds a week? That's very good.
　　　A. hundred of　　B. hundreds of　　　C. hundreds　　　　D. hundred

(　　) 7. There are _____ students in our school.
　　　A. three thousand　　　　　　　B. three thousand of
　　　C. three thousands　　　　　　　D. three thousands of

(　　) 8. We have a band in our school. _____ of the singers are from our class. They are David Brown, James Green and Lucy King.
　　　A. Six　　　　B. Sixth　　　　C. Three　　　　D. Third

(　　) 9. He was doing some washing _____.
　　　A. at eight yesterday morning　　　B. yesterday morning eight
　　　C. yesterday morning at eight　　　D. by eight yesterday morning

(　　) 10. Every day he begins to do his homework _____.
　　　A. at ten past seven　　　　　　B. at seven pass ten
　　　C. on ten past seventh　　　　　D. until ten

(　　) 11. My brother is in _____.
　　　A. Three Class, One Grade　　　B. Class Three, Grade One
　　　C. Grade One, Class Three　　　D. class three, grade one

(　　) 12. We are going to learn _____ this term.
　　　A. book six　　B. six book　　C. the book six　　D. Book Six

(　　) 13. Please turn to _____. Let's read the text aloud.
　　　A. Page Two　　　　　　　　　B. the page two
　　　C. second page　　　　　　　　D. page second

(　　) 14. There are _____ days in a year.
　　　A. three hundreds sixty-five　　　B. three hundreds and sixty-five
　　　C. three hundred and sixty-five　　D. three hundred and sixty five

(　　) 15. _____ people visit this museum every day.
　　　A. Hundred　　B. Hundreds　　C. Hundred of　　D. Hundreds of

(　　) 16. _____ trees have been planted in our school in the past 10 years.
　　　A. Thousands of　　　　　　　　B. Two thousands
　　　C. Thousand of　　　　　　　　D. Two thousand of

(　　) 17. Look! There are _____ in the sky.
　　　A. thousand stars　　　　　　　B. thousand of stars
　　　C. thousands of stars　　　　　　D. thousands of star

(   ) 18. They moved to Beijing _____ .
        A. in 1980s   B. in the 1980'
        C. in the 1980s   D. on the 1980's

(   ) 19. Sunday is the _____ day of the week.
        A. seventh   B. first   C. second   D. third

(   ) 20. _____ of the students are girls in our class.
        A. Two three   B. Two threes
        C. Two thirds   D. Second three

第七节　介词

一、介词的定义

介词（preposition 简称 prep.）又称作前置词，表示名词、代词等与句中其他词的关系，在句中不能单独作句子成分。介词后面一般有名词、代词或相当于名词的其他词类、短语或从句作它的宾语，表示与其他成分的关系。介词和它的宾语构成介词词组。

二、介词的分类

1. 简单介词，如：in, on, with, by, for, at, about, under, of 等。

2. 合成介词，如：into, within, throughout, inside, outside, without 等。

3. 重叠介词，如：from among 从……当中，from behind 从……后面，until after 直至……之后，at about 在大约……，after about 在大约……之后等。

4. 短语介词即一个或两个简单介词和一个或几个其他词类构成一个短语，作用相当于一个介词。这类介词的末尾总是一个简单介词。

如：according to, because of, by means of, in addition to, in front of, in spite of 等。

三、常用介词的区别

1. 表示在某时间，常用介词有 at, on, in 等。

（1）用 at 来表示在某一时刻。

at dawn/daybreak：在黎明

at six：在 6 点钟

at midnight：在午夜

at 4：30：在 4 点 30 分

用 at 来表示在……岁时

at sixteen/at the age of sixteen：16 岁的时候

（2）用 on 来表示在星期几/某日。

on Monday：在星期一

on January fifth：在 1 月 5 日

on Christmas Day：在圣诞节那一天，也可用 at Christmas

on New Year's Day：在新年那天

（3）用 in 来表示一天中的早中晚、月份、季节或年份。

in the morning/afternoon/evening 在早上/下午/晚上

in January/February 在一月/二月

in Spring 在春天

in 2014 在 2014 年

2. 表示期间，常用介词有 during, for, over, within, throughout, from 和 to 等。

（1）During 在……期间；在……期间的某个时候。

during the Middle Ages：在中世纪

during 1942：在 1942 年中

during the summer（of that year：在（那一年的）夏季）

during his childhood：在他童年时期

（2）for 用来表示一段时间。

for six years：六年之久

for two months：有两个月

for ever：永远

3. 表示方位，常用介词有 at, in, on, to, for 等。

（1）at：表示在小地方；表示"在……附近，旁边"。

（2）in 表示在大地方；表示"在……范围之内"。

（3）on 表示毗邻，接壤，"在……上面"。

（4）to 表示在……范围外，不强调是否接壤；或"到……"。

（5）above, over, on 在……上。

above 指在……上方，不强调是否垂直，与 below 相对

over 指垂直的上方，与 under 相对，但 over 与物体有一定的空间，不直接接触

on 表示某物体上面并与之接触

The bird is flying above my head.

鸟儿从我的头上飞过。

There is a bridge over the river.

横跨河上的大桥。

He put his watch on the desk.

他把手表放在桌子上。

（6）below, under 在……下面。

under 表示在……正下方

below 表示在……下，不一定在正下方

There is a cat under the table.

桌子下面有一只猫。

Please write your name below the line.

请把你的名字写在横线下面。

（7）in front of, in the front of 在……前面。

in front of…… 意思是"在……前面",指甲物在乙物之前,两者互不包括;其反义词是 behind(在……的后面)

There are some flowers in front of the house.

房子前面有些花卉。

in the front of 意思是"在……的前部",即甲物在乙物的前部。反义词是 at the back of…(在…范围内的后部)。

There is a blackboard in the front of our classroom.

我们的教室前边有一块黑板。

Our teacher stands in the front of the classroom.

我们的老师站在教室前。(老师在教室里)

(8) beside, behind：beside 表示在……旁边；behind 表示在……后面。

4. 表示进行。

He is at work. 他正在工作。

The house is on fire! 房子着火了!

The road is under construction. 路正在修。

真题分析

1. I always play basketball _____ Saturdays.
   A. on　　　　　　B. in　　　　　　C. at　　　　　　D. by

   分析：我总是在周六打篮球。由句意可知,是指"在星期六",在星期几的前面介词用 on,故答案选 A。

2. Humans can not make progress _____ dreams.
   A. with　　　　　B. without　　　　C. through　　　　D. about

   分析：没有了梦想,人类就不会进步。A. 带着,有；B. 没有；C. 通过；D. 关于。梦想是人类前进的动力,根据 Humans can not make progress,可知人类不会进步,是因为没有梦想,应会使用介词 without,故答案是 B。

3. It's very important _____ us to make a plan before a new term begins.
   A. of　　　　　　B. with　　　　　C. by　　　　　　D. for

   分析：对我们而言,在新学期开始之前制订计划是很重要的。of,……的；with 和……一起；for 为了；by 通过。It's + 形容词 + for/of sb. to do sth. ,对某人来说做某事是……的,固定句型,当其前形容词是描述事物特征时,用 for,当其前的形容词是描述人的品行特征时,如 nice, kind, clever, foolish, smart 都是形容人品行特征的,用 of,此处描述制订计划这件事很重要,表示事物特征,空格处应用 for,故答案选 D。

4. Let's take a walk _____ the river after diner, shall we?
   A. along　　　　　B. through　　　　C. upon　　　　　D. over

   分析：我们晚饭后沿着河散步,好吗? A. 沿着；B. 穿过；C. 根据；D. 在……正上方。根据常识可知沿着河散步, along the river,沿着河,固定搭配,故选 A。

5. Jimmy and his parents visited us _____ a cold night last winter.
   A. at　　　　　　B. in　　　　　　C. of　　　　　　D. on

分析： 在去年冬天一个寒冷的夜晚，吉米和他的父母来拜访我们。at 后跟时间点；in + 世纪、年、季节、月份等或 + 早晨、下午、晚上；of……的（表示所属）；on + 具体到某一天的时间或具体某一天的早晨、下午、晚上。根据空后 a cold night last winter 可知是具体某天的晚上，用 on，故选 D。

实战演练

( ) 1. The weather is too cold _____ March this year.
　　　A. for　　　B. in　　　C. in　　　D. for

( ) 2. Just walk down this road and you'll see the museum _____ your right.
　　　A. on　　　B. in　　　C. at　　　D. by

( ) 3. Could I have an early morning call _____ six o'clock tomorrow?
　　　A. on　　　B. to　　　C. at　　　D. in

( ) 4. There is a telephone _____ the room.
　　　A. on　　　B. in　　　C. from　　　D. out

( ) 5. Flowers usually come out _____ spring every year.
　　　A. in　　　B. at　　　C. on　　　D. of

( ) 6. Tony gets up early in the morning. He likes to make breakfast _____ his family.
　　　A. at　　　B. on　　　C. for　　　D. from

( ) 7. —It's necessary for us to take exercise every day.
　　　—Yes. And we should go _____ bed early.
　　　A. on　　　B. with　　　C. in　　　D. to

( ) 8. We go to school _____ 7：00 _____ the morning.
　　　A. on；in　　　B. at；in　　　C. on；at　　　D. in；at

( ) 9. Betty got many gifts from her friends _____ her fifteenth birthday.
　　　A. in　　　B. at　　　C. of　　　D. on

( ) 10. —Have you seen the notice _____ the wall?
　　　—Yes, I have.
　　　A. in　　　B. on　　　C. from　　　D. to

( ) 11. —Where is Jenny?
　　　—She must be _____ the reading room. She likes reading a lot.
　　　A. on　　　B. in　　　C. to　　　D. of

( ) 12. Smoking is not good _____ you because it can affect your health.
　　　A. for　　　B. at　　　C. to　　　D. on

( ) 13. Li Na won the tennis match in France _____ June 4th, 2011.
　　　A. in　　　B. on　　　C. at　　　D. for

( ) 14. —How do you go home every day?
　　　—_____ bike. It's not far from here.
　　　A. On　　　B. In　　　C. By　　　D. With

( ) 15. John and Tom come _____ Canada.

| | A. with | B. in | C. from | D. for |

( ) 16. My mother said she would come _____ Saturday morning.
　　　　 A. in　　　　 B. to　　　　　　 C. on　　　　　　　　　 D. with

( ) 17. Neil Armstrong was the first man to walk on the moon _____ 1969.
　　　　 A. in　　　　 B. at　　　　　　 C. for　　　　　　　　　D. on

( ) 18. More and more young people go swimming _____ summer.
　　　　 A. at　　　　 B. in　　　　　　 C. on　　　　　　　　　 D. to

( ) 19. Jimmy is coming to Beijing by plane. I'll meet him _____ the airport tomorrow.
　　　　 A. on　　　　 B. at　　　　　　 C. off　　　　　　　　　D. for

( ) 20. —When did the car accident happen?
　　　　 —It happened _____ a rainy night.
　　　　 A. at　　　　 B. on　　　　　　 C. in　　　　　　　　　 D. to

第八节　连词

一、连词的定义

连词（conjunction 简称 conj.）是一种虚词，用于连接单词、短语或句子，在句子中不单独用作句子成分。连词按其性质可分为并列连词和从属连词。并列连词用于连接并列的单词、短语或句子，如 and，but，or，for 等；从属连词主要引出名词性从句（主语从句、宾语从句、表语从句等）和状语从句（时间状语从句、条件状语从句、目的状语从句等），引出名词性从句的连词如 that，whether 等，引出状语从句的连词如 when，because，since，if 等。

二、并列连词的用法

1. 表示转折关系的并列连词。这类连词主要有 but，yet 等。如：
Someone borrowed my pen, but I don't remember who.
有人借了我的钢笔，但我不记得是谁了。
He said he was our friend, yet he wouldn't help us.
他说他是我们的朋友，却不肯帮助我们。
2. 表示因果关系的并列连词。这类连词主要有 for，so 等。如：
The child had a bad cough, so his mother took him to the doctor.
这孩子咳得很厉害，所以他妈妈带他去看医生。
You are supposed to get rid of carelessness, for it often leads to serious errors.
你们一定要克服粗枝大叶，因为粗枝大叶常常引起严重的错误。
注意：for 表示结果通常不能放句首，也不能单独使用。
3. 表示并列关系的并列连词。这类连词主要有 and，or，either…or，neither…nor，not only…but（also），both…and，as well as 等。如：
He didn't go and she didn't go either.

他没去，她也没去。
The weather is mild today; it is neither hot nor cold.
今天天气很温暖，不冷也不热。
Both New York and London have traffic problems.
纽约和伦敦都存在交通问题。
It is important for you as well as for me.
这对你和对我都很重要。
People who are either under age or over age may not join the army.
年龄不到或者超龄的人都不得参军。

三、从属连词的用法

1. 引导时间状语从句的从属连词。

（1）表示"当……时候"或"每当"的时间连词。这类连词主要有 when, while, as, whenever，如：

Don't talk while you're eating.
吃饭时不要说话。
Vegetables are best when they are fresh.
蔬菜新鲜时最好吃。
He came just as I was leaving.
我正要走时他来了。

（2）表示"在……之前（或之后）"的时间连词。这类连词主要有 before, after，如：

Try to finish your work before you leave.
离开前设法把工作做完。
After we have finished tea, we will sit on the grass.
喝完茶之后我们将坐在草地上。

（3）表示"自从"或"直到"的时间连词。这类连词主要有 since, until, till，如：

She's been playing tennis since she was eight.
她从八岁起就打网球了。
Hold on until I fetch help.
坚持一下，等我找人来帮忙。
Never trouble trouble till trouble troubles you.
（谚）不要无事惹事。

（4）表示"一……就……"的时间连词。这类连词主要有 as soon as, the moment, the minute, the second, the instant, immediately, directly, instantly, once, no sooner...than, hardly...when 等，如：

I'll let you know as soon as I hear from her.
我一接到她的信就通知你。
The moment I have finished I'll give you a call.
我一干完就给你打电话。

I came immediately I heard the news.
我一听到这个消息，马上就来了。
Once you begin you must continue.
你一旦开始，便不可停下来。

（5）表示"上次""下次""每次"等的时间连词，主要有 every time（每次），each time（每次），(the) next time（下次），any time（随时），(the) last time（上次），the first time（第一次），如：

I'll tell him about it (the) next time I see him.
我下一次见到他时，我就把这个情况告诉他。
We lose a few skin cells every time we wash our hands.
每当我们洗手的时候，我们都要损失一些皮肤细胞。
You can call me any time you want to.
你随时都可以给我打电话。

注意：every time, each time, any time 前不用冠词，(the) next time, (the) last time 中的冠词可以省略，而 the first time 中的冠词通常不能省略。

2. 引导条件状语从句的从属连词。这类连词主要有 if, unless, as/so long as, in case 等，如：

Do you mind if I open the window?
我开窗你不介意吧？
Don't come unless I telephone.
除非我打电话，否则你别来。
As long as you're happy, it doesn't matter what you do.
只要你高兴，你做什么都没关系。
In case it rains they will stay at home.
万一下雨，他们就待在家里。

注意：在条件状语从句中，通常要用一般现在时表示将来意义，而不能直接使用将来时态。

3. 引导目的状语从句的从属连词。这类连词主要有 in order that, so that, in case, for fear 等，如：

He raised his voice so that everyone could hear it.
他提高了嗓音，以便每个人都能听见。
Take your umbrella (just) in case it rains.
带上雨伞，以防下雨。
She repeated the instructions slowly in order that he should understand.
她把那些指示慢慢重复了一遍好让他听明白。

4. 引导结果状语从句的从属连词。这类连词主要有 so that, so...that, such...that 等，如：

I went to the lecture early so that I got a good seat.
我去听演讲去得很早，所以找了个好座位。

I had so many falls that I was black and blue all over.

我摔了许多跤，以致全身都是青一块紫一块的。

He shut the window with such force that the glass broke.

他关窗用力很大，结果玻璃震破了。

5. 引导原因状语从句的从属连词。这类连词主要有 because, as, since, seeing (that), now (that), considering (that) 等，如：

He distrusted me because I was new.

他不信任我，因为我是新来的。

As you are sorry, I'll forgive you.

既然你悔悟了，我就原谅你。

Since we've no money, we can't buy it.

由于我们没钱，我们无法购买它。

Seeing that he's ill he's unlikely to come.

因为他病了，他大概不会来了。

Now that she has apologized, I am content.

既然她已经道了歉，我也就满意了。

6. 引导让步状语从句的从属连词。这类连词主要有 although, though, even though, even if, while, however, whatever, whoever, whenever, wherever 等，如：

Although they are twins, they look entirely different.

他们虽是孪生，但是相貌却完全不同。

I like her even though she can be annoying.

尽管她有时很恼人，但我还是喜欢她。

You won't move that stone, however strong you are.

不管你力气多大，也休想搬动那块石头。

Whatever we have achieved, we owe to your support.

我们取得的一切成就都归功于你们的支持。

Whoever you are, you can't pass this way.

不管你是谁，你都不能从这里通过。

Whenever I see him, I speak to him.

每当我见到他，我都和他讲话。

7. 引导方式状语从句的从属连词。这类连词主要有 as, as if, as though, the way 等，如：

Why didn't you catch the last bus as I told you to?

你怎么不听我的话赶乘末班公共汽车呢？

He bent the iron bar as if it had been made of rubber.

他将铁棍折弯，仿佛那是用橡皮做成的。

Nobody else loves you the way (＝as) I do.

没有人像我这样爱你。

8. 引导地点状语从句的从属连词。这类连词主要有 where, wherever, everywhere, anywhere 等，如：

The church was built where there had once been a Roman temple.

这座教堂盖在一座罗马寺庙的旧址。

I'll take you anywhere you like.

你想到哪儿我就带你到哪儿。

Everywhere I go, I find the same thing.

不管我走到哪里，我都会发现同样情况。

9. 引导比较状语从句的从属连词。这类连词主要有 than 和 as...as，如：

She was now happier than she had ever been.

现在她比过去任何时候都快活。

I glanced at my watch. It was earlier than I thought.

我看了看表，时间比我想象的早。

He doesn't work as hard as she does.

他工作不像她那样努力。

10. 引起名词从句的从属连词。这类连词主要有 that, whether, if 等，它们用于引导主语从句、表语从句、宾语从句和同位语从句。其中 that 不充当句子成分，而且没有词义，在句子中只起连接作用；而 if, whether 虽不充当句子成分，但有词义，即表示"是否"。如：

He replied that he was going by train.

他回答说他将坐火车去。

I wonder if it's large enough.

我不知道它是否够大。

I worry about whether I hurt her feelings.

我为是否伤了她的感情而担心。

真题分析

1. You aren't able to lose weight _____ you change your eating habits.
   A. if B. unless C. after D. since

   分析：除非你改变你的饮食习惯，否则你不能减肥。A. 如果；B. 除非……；C. 在……之后；D. 自从。除非改变饮食习惯，否则不能减肥，所以用 unless，故选 B。

2. Cathy is afraid of the dog. She will run away _____ she sees it.
   A. ever since B. although C. as soon as D. so that

   分析：凯西害怕狗。她一看见狗就逃走。A. 自从；B. 虽然、即使；C. 一……就……；D. 以便。这是一个主从复合句，挖空处后引导一个时间状语从句，连词用 as soon as，一……就……，故选 C。

3. The Great Wall is _____ famous _____ lots of visitors all over the world come to visit it every year.
   A. so; that B. such; that C. enough; that D. very; that

   分析：长城是如此著名，以至于每年都有许多世界各地的游客来参观它。enough 和 very 不引导从句，故 C, D 选项被排除，so + 形容词 + that，引导结果状语从句，such + 名词+that，引导结果状语从句，famous 是形容词，故选 A。

4. Tony has learned a lot about Chinese culture _____ he came to China.
   A. before   B. since   C. until   D. when
   分析：自从来到中国，托尼学到很多关于中国文化的东西。before 在……之前；since 自从，后跟表示过去的时间状语和现在完成时连用；until 直到……才……，不和完成时连用；when 当……时候，和过去完成时连用。故选 B。

5. Jenny didn't go to bed _____ her mother came home last night.
   A. as soon as   B. if   C. while   D. until
   分析：昨天晚上珍妮直到母亲回家才睡觉。as soon as，一……就……；if，如果；while，当……时候；until，直到，not...until...，直到……才……，故选 D。

实战演练

( ) 1. We hope to go to the beach tomorrow, but we won't go _____ it rains.
   A. if   B. when   C. though   D. because

( ) 2. You should buy a map _____ you travel to a new city.
   A. as   B. after   C. as soon as   D. before

( ) 3. —Would you like to come to my house for dinner this evening?
   —I'd love to, _____ I am too busy.
   A. so   B. and   C. but   D. or

( ) 4. He didn't go to work yesterday _____ he was ill.
   A. where   B. how   C. because   D. if

( ) 5. It's windy outside. Put on your coat, _____ you may catch a cold.
   A. and   B. but   C. or   D. so

( ) 6. —Mom, shall we have supper now?
   —Oh, we won't have supper _____ your dad comes back.
   A. until   B. since   C. while   D. after

( ) 7. Cross the road carefully, _____ you'll keep yourself safe.
   A. and   B. or   C. but   D. though

( ) 8. —Shall we get off the bus here?
   —Yes. But we won't get off _____ it stops.
   A. when   B. until   C. while   D. after

( ) 9. _____ the mother was cooking in the kitchen, the baby fell asleep in the chair.
   A. Since   B. While   C. Because   D. Once

( ) 10. Mom won't let Dick go out _____ he promises to be back by 10：00 tonight.
   A. if   B. when   C. since   D. unless

( ) 11. He didn't go to school yesterday _____ he was ill.
   A. because   B. because of   C. if   D. so

( ) 12. The teacher speaks very loudly _____ all the students can hear her.
   A. so that   B. because   C. since   D. when

(   ) 13. My room is small, _____ it is comfortable.
　　　　　A. and　　　　B. or　　　　　　C. but　　　　　　D. so

(   ) 14. We'll plant trees tomorrow, and I don't know _____ Tom will come and join us.
　　　　　A. if　　　　B. which　　　　C. what　　　　D. where

(   ) 15. A snake bit (咬) him, _____ he went to see a doctor at once.
　　　　　A. if　　　　B. where　　　　C. because　　　　D. so

(   ) 16. The writer walked slowly _____ his bad leg.
　　　　　A. because　　B. since　　　　C. as　　　　　　D. because of

(   ) 17. The beginning of the movie was boring, _____ the end was amazing!
　　　　　A. but　　　　B. and　　　　　C. so　　　　　　D. or

(   ) 18. _____ I had walked for six hours, I was tired out.
　　　　　A. After　　　B. Before　　　　C. When　　　　D. As

(   ) 19. You may borrow this book _____ you promise to give it back.
　　　　　A. in case　　B. so long as　　C. as if　　　　D. even if

(   ) 20. _____ you understand this rule, you'll have no further difficulty.
　　　　　A. Once　　　B. Unless　　　　C. As　　　　　D. Until

第九节　动词

一、动词的定义

动词（verb 简称 v.）是用来表示动作或状态的词，如 walk，laugh，have，lie，see，write，fly，start，wake 等。动词通常充当句子的谓语，表示主语的动作、存在、变化，或主语对宾语的动作或态度。

二、动词的分类

按照动词的意义可以分为实义动词、连系动词、助动词和情态动词。
1. 实义动词词义完整，能独立作谓语，可分成及物动词和不及物动词。
（1）及物动词要求有宾语。
①Mr. Smith gave his wife twenty pounds for her birthday.
史密斯先生给了他的妻子20英镑过生日。
②She asked the teacher a few questions.
她向老师问了几个问题。
③We have friends all over the world.
我们的朋友遍天下。
④Children and young people like bright colors.
孩子和年轻人喜欢亮丽的颜色。
（2）不及物动词不要求有宾语。
①Most shops in Britain open at 9：00 a. m. and close at 5：00 or 5：30 in the evening.

英国大部分商店上午九点开门，晚五点或五点半关门。
②George's father lives there.
乔治的爸爸住在那里。
③Let's go home.
我们回家吧。
④The examination ended at 11：30 a.m.
考试上午十一点半结束。
2. 连系动词。
连系动词有些不具有词义，有些具有词义，但不能单独用作谓语，后边必须跟表语构成系表结构说明主语的状况、性质、特征等情况。
（1）状态系动词。
用来表示主语状态，只有 be 一词，如：
He is a teacher.
他是一名教师。
（2）持续系动词。
用来表示主语继续或保持一种状况或态度，主要有 keep, rest, remain, stay, lie, stand, 如：
He always kept silent at meeting.
他开会时总保持沉默。
This matter rests a mystery.
此事仍是一个谜。
（3）表像系动词。
用来表示"看起来像"这一概念，主要有 seem, appear, 如：
He seems (to be) very sad.
他看起来很伤心。
（4）感官系动词。
感官系动词主要有 feel, look, smell, sound, taste, 如：
This kind of cloth feels very soft.
这种布手感很软。
He looks tired.
他看起来很累。
This flower smells very sweet.
这朵花闻起来很香。
（5）变化系动词。
这些系动词表示主语变成什么样，变化系动词主要有 become, grow, turn, fall, get, go, come, run, 如：
He became mad after that.
自那之后，他疯了。
She grew rich within a short time.

她没多长时间就富了。

3. 助动词。

常用的助动词有：be，have，do，shall，will，should，would。协助主要动词构成谓语动词词组的词叫助动词，被协助的动词称作主要动词，助动词自身没有词义，不可单独使用，如：

He doesn't like English.

他不喜欢英语。

（doesn't 是助动词，无词义；like 是主要动词，有词义）

助动词协助主要动词完成以下功能，可以用来：

（1）表示时态，如：

He is singing.

他在唱歌。

He has got married.

他已结婚。

（2）表示语态，如：

He was sent to England.

他被派往英国。

（3）构成疑问句，如：

Do you like college life?

你喜欢大学生活吗？

Did you study English before you came here?

你来这儿之前学过英语吗？

（4）与否定副词 not 合用，构成否定句，如：

I don't like him. 我不喜欢他。

（5）加强语气，如：

Do come to the party tomorrow evening.

明天晚上一定来参加晚会。

He did know that.

他的确知道那件事。

4. 情态动词。

常见的情态动词有 can，may，must，shall，will，need 等；另外，have to，had better 也当作情态动词使用。情态动词后面必须加动词的原形。

（1）表示"可能、许可、能力"（can/could，may/might）。can 表示已经发生的事实再次发生的可能性；may/might 表示未知的可能性。can/could 表示"能力"时，通常可以和 be able to 互换；但表示将来具有的能力或是过去有能力并成功做了某事时，只能用 be able to。

Can you lift this heavy box?

你能举起这个盒子吗？

Could I come to see you tomorrow?

明天我能来看你吗?

This hall can hold 500 people at least.

这个大厅至少能容纳 500 人。

—May/Might I take this book out of the room?

—我可以把这本书带出房间吗?

—No, you mustn't.

—不可以。

(2) 表示"必须"(must, have to)。must 用来指一般现在时和一般将来时；过去时可用 have to 的过去时代替。must 表示主观思想；have to 表示客观需要。mustn't 表示"禁止"，not have to 表示"不必"。

You must come on time.

你必须按时来。

I had to do my homework last night, so I couldn't go shopping with you.

昨晚我不得不做作业，所以我不能和你去买东西。

—Must we hand in our exercise books today?

—我们今天必须交练习本吗?

—Yes, you must.

—是的，必须交。

—No, you don't have to/you needn't.

—不，不必交。

(3) dare 表示"敢于……"，主要用于否定句或疑问句中。

How dare you say I'm unfair?

你敢说我不公平吗?

If we dared not go there that day, we couldn't get the beautiful flowers.

如果我们那天不敢去那里，我们就不能得到美丽的花。

(4) need 作情态动词用时，常用于疑问句、否定句。在肯定句中一般用 must, have to, ought to, should 代替。

You needn't come so early.

你不必来这么早。

Need I finish the work today?

我需要今天完成这项工作吗?

(5) shall 表示"建议"。

Shall we go to the park?

我们去公园好吗?

What shall we do this evening?

今天晚上我们做什么?

(6) 表示"意愿或习惯"(will/would, shall/ should)。

I will never do that again.

我再也不会那样做了。

They asked him if he would go abroad.

他们问他是否愿意出国。

During the vacation, he would visit me every other day.

在假期里,他每隔一天来看我一次。

The wound would not heal.

伤口不愈合。

I should help her because she is in trouble.

我应该帮助她,因为她遇到了麻烦。

真题分析

1. _____ late again, Bill!
   A. Don't to be   B. Don't be   C. Not be   D. Be not

   分析:比尔,不要再迟到了。本句为祈使句的否定句,祈使句的否定句是以 don't 开始,后面跟动词原形,故选 B。

2. The boy is sleeping. Please _____ the radio.
   A. turn up   B. turn down   C. turn on   D. turn around

   分析:A. turn up 增大,调高;B. turn down 减小,调低;C. turn on 打开;D. turn around 转身。句意:那个男孩正在睡觉,请_____收音机。故选 B。

3. Mom is making dinner. It _____ so nice!
   A. smells   B. tastes   C. feels   D. sounds

   分析:妈妈在做饭,闻起来如此香。A. smells 闻起来;B. tastes 尝起来;C. feels 感觉,摸起来;D. sounds 听起来。闻到了食物的香味,闻起来,故选 A。

4. —Can your sister _____ volleyball?
   —Yes, she can. But she _____ play it very well.
   A. playing; can't   B. playing; can   C. play; can't   D. play; can

   分析:——你姐姐会打排球吗?——是的,她会。但是她打得不好。Can 后跟动词原形;but 表示转折,故在本题中 but 引导的应是否定句。故选 C。

5. — Must I clean the room now, Mr. White?
   —No, you _____.
   A. shouldn't   B. needn't   C. wouldn't   D. can't

   分析:——怀特先生,我必须现在打扫房间吗?——不,没有必要。A. shouldn't "不应该";B. needn't "不必";C. wouldn't "不会";D. can't "不能"。一般疑问句"Must…?"的肯定答语为 Yes, …must. 否定答语为 No, …needn't. 故选 B。

实战演练

( ) 1. _____ everyone here today?
   A. Be   B. Are   C. Is   D. Am

( ) 2. Harry is older than I. But he _____ younger than I.
   A. look   B. looks   C. looked   D. looking

( ) 3. It _____ like the singing of the birds.
   A. sounds   B. looks   C. smells   D. tastes

( ) 4. This kind of cake tastes _____.
   A. good   B. well   C. to be good   D. to be well

( ) 5. This kind of paper _____ nice.
   A. feel   B. felt   C. is feeling   D. feels

( ) 6. Coffee is ready. How nice it _____! Would you like some?
   A. looks   B. smells   C. sounds   D. feels

( ) 7. John always _____ others.
   A. help   B. helping   C. helps   D. to help

( ) 8. He _____ for eight hours every day.
   A. working   B. to work   C. works   D. worked

( ) 9. In winter the days _____ colder and colder.
   A. gets   B. getting   C. got   D. get

( ) 10. _____ you tell me what's happening over there?
   A. Could   B. May   C. Might   D. Shall

( ) 11. _____ I have a word with the manager, sir?
   A. Will   B. Would   C. May   D. Can

( ) 12. If it is fine tomorrow, we _____ a football match.
   A. have   B. will have   C. has   D. shall has

( ) 13. I _____ go to bed until I _____ finished my work.
   A. don't; had
   B. didn't; have
   C. didn't; had
   D. don't; have

( ) 14. No one _____ that to his face.
   A. dares say
   B. dares saying
   C. dare say
   D. dare to say

( ) 15. There _____ an English film at the cinema now.
   A. will have
   B. is going to have
   C. is going to be
   D. is

( ) 16. The teacher _____ us to come to school on time.
   A. ask   B. asking   C. asks   D. asked

( ) 17. You'd better _____ at home and _____ your homework.
   A. to stay, do
   B. stay, do
   C. to stay, to do
   D. stay, to do

( ) 18. Uncle Wang never _____ a cake.
   A. make   B. to make   C. making   D. makes

( ) 19. Look. They _____ a good time, _____ they?
   A. have, do
   B. have, don't
   C. are having, are
   D. are having, aren't

(　　) 20. The teacher _____ when I came into the classroom.
　　A. is drawing　　　　　　　B. draws
　　C. has drawn　　　　　　　D. was drawing

第十节　动词时态

英语中不同时间和方式发生的动作或状态要用谓语动词的不同形式来表示，这种表示动作或状态发生时间和方式的动词形式称作动词时态。常用的时态有一般现在时、现在进行时、一般过去时、过去进行时、一般将来时、过去将来时、现在完成时、过去完成时等。

一般现在时

一、概述

表示经常性、规律性、习惯性的状态或者动作，常与 every，always，often，usually，sometimes 等表示现在时间的状语连用。

二、基本结构

一般现在时主要由动词原形表示，如果主语是第三人称单数，则在动词原形后加-s 或 -es，词尾读音分别为［s］，［z］或［iz］。

三、一般现在时的用法

1. 表示经常或习惯性的动作，或现在存在的状态（能力、特征、职务、身份、籍贯等），一般现在时常与 every day（week，month，year…），usually，often，sometimes，always 等连用。

She speaks English very well.
她英语讲得很好。

2. 表示永恒的状态或真理。

The earth moves round the sun.
地球绕太阳运转。

3. 动词 go，come，start，begin，leave，arrive，return，be 等的一般现在时可用来代替将来时，表示事先已按计划安排好的将要发生的动作或状态。

The new TV play begins at 5：15 this afternoon.
新电视剧将在今天下午五点一刻开始。

4. 动词 say，learn 等的一般现在时可用来代替现在完成时。

She says they will read more English books this term.
她说这学期他们要多读英语方面的书籍。

现在进行时

一、概述

表示现在（指说话人说话时）正在进行的动作，常与 now 连用。

二、基本结构

be（am，is，are）+ v-ing（现在分词）。

三、现在进行时的基本用法

1. 表示现在（指说话人说话时）正在发生的事情。
We are waiting for you.
我们正等你呢。
2. 表示长期的或重复性的动作，说话时动作未必正在进行。
Mr. Green is writing another novel.
格林先生在写另一部小说。
（说话时并未在写，只处于写作的状态。）
3. 已经确定或安排好的将来活动。
We're flying to Paris tomorrow.
我们明天乘飞机去巴黎。
I'm leaving for a trip in Nepal next week.
我下周要去尼泊尔旅行。
4. 在时间或条件状语从句中，要用现在进行时表示将来进行时。
If they are having a meeting when I get there this afternoon, I'll wait for them in the office.
今天下午我去他们那儿时，如果他们开会，我就在办公室等。
5. 表示瞬间动作的动词，如 go，come，start，leave，arrive 等，可用现在进行时表示即将发生的将来动作。
The train is arriving.
火车要到了。

一般过去时

一、概述

表示过去某个时间发生的动作或存在的状态，常与 yesterday，ago，last week 等表示过去时间的状语连用。

二、基本结构

一般过去时主要由动词的过去式表示。

三、一般过去时的基本用法

1. 表示过去某一时间内发生的动作或存在的状态，常与表示过去时间的状语 yesterday, last week, half an hour ago, in 2019 等连用。

—Where were you yesterday? —I was at home.
昨天你在哪儿？　　　　　　　在家呀。

2. 表示过去某一时间内连续发生的几种动作。

At half past seven, he stood up, turned off his TV set and then went out.
七点半，他站起来，关掉电视机，然后出去了。

3. 表示过去某一时间内经常的或习惯性的动作或状态。

When we were in Grade Two, we always got up early.
我上二年级时，总是早早起床。

4. 在时间及条件状语从句中，要用一般过去时表示过去将来时。

Tom said he would go shopping when his mother came back.
汤姆说他妈妈一回来，他就去买东西。

过去进行时

一、概述

表示过去某个时刻或某个阶段正在发生的动作，常与 then, this time 等时间状语连用。

二、基本结构

be（was，were）+ v-ing（现在分词）。

三、过去进行时的基本用法

1. 表示在过去某一时刻或过去某一阶段正在进行的动作。

They were having a good time in the park this time yesterday.
昨天这时候他们正在公园玩得高兴呢。

2. 瞬间动词如 go, come, start, leave, arrive, die 等的过去进行时可以表示过去即将发生的动作。

We wanted to tell her that we were not going there again the next week.
我们想告诉她下周不去那儿了。

3. 当两个动作在过去某一时间同时发生时，用过去进行时表示延续性动作。过去进行时可用于主句，也可用于从句。

It was raining hard when I left my office.
我离开办公室时，雨下得正大。

一般将来时

一、概述

一般表示将来某个时间要发生的动作或存在的状态

二、基本结构

一般将来时由"will/shall + 动词原形或 is/am/are going to + 动词原形"构成。will 用于第二、第三人称，shall 用于第一人称。

三、一般将来时的基本用法

1. shall/will + 动词原形表示将要发生的动作或存在状态，常与表示将来的时间状语连用，如 tomorrow, next Sunday, soon, in a month, in the future 等。

My younger brother will be fifteen years old next year.
我弟弟明年就 15 岁了。
What shall we do if he doesn't come?
如果他不来，我们该怎么办？
Will you be free this evening?
今天晚上有空吗？
I think he will tell us the truth.
我想他会告诉我们真实情况的。

2. is/am/are going to + 动词原形表示打算做某事或有迹象表明即将发生某事。

We are going to sail around the small island.
我们打算绕着小岛航行。
They are going to have a meeting to discuss the matter this evening.
他们今天晚上开会讨论这件事情。
Look at the black clouds over there. I think it is going to rain soon.
看一看那边的乌云，我想天要下雨了。
There is going to be an English evening this week.
本周要举行一个英语晚会。

3. is/am/are + to 动词原形常表示按安排、计划、约定或要求将要发生的动作。

Your assignment is to be handed in next Monday.
你的作业下周一必须上交。
Our headmaster is to attend a national academic conference in April.
我们校长将在四月参加一个全国性的学术会议。
Who is to clean the classroom today?
今天该谁打扫教室了？
When are you to return your library book?
你什么时候要还图书？

4. is/am/are about + to do 表示即将发生的动作，不可接时间状语。
We are about to leave, so there is no time to visit the palace.
我们就要离开了，因此没有时间去参观那座宫殿了。
Don't leave. Li Lei is about to come.
不要走了，李雷就要来了。
Be quiet. The concert is about to start.
安静下来，音乐演唱会就要开始了。
Mr. Wang was about to leave his office when the telephone rang.
王先生正要离开办公室，这时电话响了。
5. is/am/are + 动词现在分词（仅限位移动词 go, come, leave, start, arrive 等）常表示按计划、安排将要发生某事。
They are leaving school in one year.
他们一年之后要毕业了。
Go ahead, and I'm coming.
往前面走吧，我就来。
You are seeking for a job after graduation.
毕业后你们就要找工作。

过去将来时

一、概述

过去将来时表示从过去某时看来将要发生的动作或存在的状态。

二、基本结构

would/should + 动词原形或 was/were going to + 动词原形。

三、过去将来时的基本用法

1. 表示从过去某个时间而言将要发生的动作或存在的状态。
He said his mother would come to see him the next day.
他说他的妈妈第二天要来看他。
I hoped that we would meet again soon.
我希望我们能很快再次相见。
I knew you were going to go to the party.
我知道你会来参加聚会的。
We all thought you would help us.
我们都觉得你会提供帮助的。
2. 表示过去的某种习惯性行为。
Mike told me he would read some books in his spare time.
迈克告诉我在空闲时间他将会读书。

When I was a young girl, I would sit, listening to music in my room.
当我还是个小女孩的时候,我会坐在房间,听着音乐。
Mum said she would wait for me on my way home at the end of every month.
妈妈说每个月末她都会在回家的路上等我。

现在完成时

一、概述

现在完成时表示过去所发生的动作或事情对现在造成的影响或产生的结果。

二、基本结构

助动词 have/has + 动词过去分词。

三、现在完成时的基本用法

1. 表示动作发生在过去,但与现在的情况有联系,有时无时间状语,有时和一些表示不确定的过去时间状语连用,强调对现在的影响,着眼点在现在,常与 already, yet, just, recently, lately, ever, never, twice 等连用。

I have just copied all the new words.
我已经抄了所有新单词。
She has never heard Jenny tell lies.
她说从来没听到过珍妮说谎。
Someone has broken the window.
有人把窗户打破了。
I have lost my pen.
我把钢笔丢了。
He has finished his work.
他已经完成了工作。
My father has gone to Shanghai.
我父亲去上海了。

2. 表示从过去某一时间开始一直延续到现在并还可能继续延续下去的动作,且句中常带有由 since 或 for 引导的表示一段时间的时间状语。

He has taught in our school for 30 years.
他在我们学校教书已有 30 年了。
I have lived here for more than twenty years.
我在这里住了 20 多年了。
Mary has been ill for three days.
玛丽已经病了 3 天了。
He has lived here since 1978.
自从 1978 年以来,他一直住在这儿。

I have learned English since I came here.
自从我来到这儿就学英语了。
Changes have taken place since you left.
自从你走后，已经发生了很大的变化。

过去完成时

一、概述

过去完成时表示过去某个时间或某个动作之前已经完成的动作，或者表示动作从过去某个时间开始一直延续到过去另一时间的动作，即动作发生在过去的过去，常用 by，before 或一个过去的时间状语或动作来表示。

二、基本结构

助动词 had + 动词过去分词。

三、过去完成时的基本用法

1. 在过去某个时间或某个动作之前已经完成的动作。

They had already finished half of the work by the end of last week.
截止到上周末他们已经完成了一半的工作。
She found she had left her handbag on the bus.
她发现已经把手提包落在了公交车上。
By nine o'clock last night, we had got 200 pictures from the spaceship.
到昨晚9点钟，我们已经收到200张飞船发来的图片。

2. 表示在过去某时开始，一直延续到过去的某个时间的动作。

By the time we left there, he had taught Chinese for 10 years.
到我们离开为止，他已经教语文课10年了。
The government had done everything it could to push down inflation.
政府已经采取了所有可能的措施来抑制通货膨胀。
Before they went to college, they had known each other for over 15 years.
在上大学之前他们已经彼此认识超过15年了。

真题分析

1. —_____ you often go to the beach?
   —No, but I _____ last Sunday.
   A. Did; want   B. Do; did   C. Did; do   D. Do, go

   分析：考查一般现在时和一般过去时；由关键词 often 看出属于一般现在时，因此助动词使用 do；由 last Sunday 看出属于一般过去时，因此使用动词过去式。故 B 项符合。

2. —May I speak to Jackie?
   —Sorry, he isn't in. He _____ a meeting.

A. have　　　　　B. had　　　　　C. is having　　　　D. to have

分析：——我可以和 Jackie 说话吗？——对不起，他不在。他正在开会。结合语境可知，本题的时态是现在进行时。故选 C。

3. —There _____ a football match this evening.
　　—Exciting news.
　　A. are going to be　　　　　　　　B. is going to be
　　C. is going to have　　　　　　　　D. will have

分析：——今天晚上有一场足球比赛。——激动人心的消息。There be 结构与将来时连用时，用 There is going to be…，不能与 have 连用，故答案为 B。

4. My grandma _____ a song with her friends when I came back.
　　A. sings　　　B. sang　　　C. is singing　　　D. was singing

分析：当我回来的时候，我的祖母正和她的朋友一起唱歌。根据 when I came back 可知此处表示过去某时正在做某事，故用过去进行时，故选 D。

5. —Where is Tom?
　　—He _____ the USA. He _____ back in two months.
　　A. has gone to; comes　　　　　　　B. has been to; will be
　　C. has been to; comes　　　　　　　D. has gone to; will be

分析：——汤姆在哪儿？——他去了美国，他将在两个月之后回来。have been to 的意思是"过去到过而现在已返回"，它强调"最近的经历"；have gone to 表示"动作的完成"，强调人已离开说话的地方。In + 一段时间，用于将来时。根据句意，故选 D。

实战演练

(　) 1. When I saw Mary, she _____ the piano.
　　　　A. is playing　　B. plays　　　C. was playing　　　D. played

(　) 2. A hunter is a man who _____ animals.
　　　　A. catch　　　B. catches　　　C. will catch　　　D. was catching

(　) 3. I will visit you if my father _____ me.
　　　　A. let　　　　B. lets　　　　C. is letting　　　　D. will let

(　) 4. Look out! That tree _____ fall down.
　　　　A. is going to　B. will be　　　C. shall　　　　　D. would

(　) 5. My uncle _____ to see me. He'll be here soon.
　　　　A. comes　　　B. is coming　　C. had come　　　　D. came

(　) 6. —Has he seen this film?
　　　　—Yes. He _____ it a few days ago.
　　　　A. saw　　　　B. has seen　　　C. had seen　　　　D. was seen

(　) 7. The sun _____ in the west.
　　　　A. falls　　　B. drops　　　C. is always setting　　D. sets

(　) 8. This bright girl _____ the truth in front of the enemy.
　　　　A. didn't say　　　　　　　　　B. couldn't speak to

C. said D. didn't tell

(　) 9. —When _____ school begin?
—Next Monday.
　　A. has　　　B. does　　　C. did　　　D. is going to

(　) 10. Now Tom _____ a book about America. I don't think he can finish it in a year.
　　A. writes　　B. has written　　C. wrote　　D. is writing

(　) 11. Each time I _____ there, I will buy him something nice.
　　A. went　　B. will go　　C. go　　D. have gone

(　) 12. We won't go unless you _____ soon.
　　A. had come　B. came　　C. will come　　D. come

(　) 13. Li Ming _____ music and often _____ to music.
　　A. like; listen　　　　　　B. likes; listens
　　C. like; are listening　　　D. liking; listen

(　) 14. He will call you if he _____ his work.
　　A. will finish　　　　B. finishes
　　C. had finished　　　D. finish

(　) 15. Whenever I _____ these days, I always carry my raincoat.
　　A. shall go out　　　B. am going out
　　C. would go out　　　D. go out

(　) 16. My brother _____ while he _____ his bicycle and hurt himself.
　　A. fell, was riding　　　B. fell, were riding
　　C. had fallen, rode　　　D. had fallen, was riding

(　) 17. She lived there before he _____ to China.
　　A. came　　B. comes　　C. come　　D. coming

(　) 18. The reporter said that the UFO _____ east to west when he saw it.
　　A. was traveling　　　B. traveled
　　C. had been traveling　　D. was to travel

(　) 19. Jenny _____ in an office. Her parents _____ in a hospital.
　　A. work; works　　　B. works; work
　　C. work; are working　D. is working; work

(　) 20. We didn't go shopping because it _____ yesterday.
　　A. don't rain　B. didn't rain　　C. rains　　D. rained

(　) 21. There _____ a meeting tomorrow afternoon.
　　A. will be going to　　B. will going to be
　　C. is going to be　　　D. will go to be

(　) 22. Miss Green isn't in the office. She _____ to the library.
　　A. has gone　B. went　　C. will go　　D. has been

(　) 23. The plane is leaving right now, but Jim hasn't arrived yet.
Well, he said he _____ here on time.

A. came　　　B. would come　　　C. can be　　　D. will be

( ) 24. Charlie _____ here next month.
A. isn't working　　　　　　B. doesn't working
C. isn't going to working　　D. won't work

( ) 25. My parents _____ Shandong for ten years.
A. have been in　　　B. have been to
C. have gone to　　　D. have been

( ) 26. As soon as the baby saw her mother, she _____.
A. was going to cry　　B. crying
C. began to cry　　　　D. was crying

( ) 27. He _____ very busy this week, he _____ free next week.
A. will be; is　　　　B. is; is
C. will be; will be　　D. is; will be

( ) 28. The students have cleaned the classroom, _____?
A. so they　　B. don't they　　C. have they　　D. haven't they

( ) 29. _____ has Mr. White been a member of Greener China since he _____ to China?
A. How soon, comes　　B. How often, got
C. How long, came　　　D. How far, arrived

( ) 30. His uncle _____ for more than 9 years.
A. has come here　　　B. has started to work
C. has lived there　　　D. has left the university

( ) 31. When Li Ming hurried home, he found that his mother _____ already _____ to hospital.
A. has; been sent　　B. had; sent
C. has; sent　　　　　D. had; been sent

( ) 32. We _____ five English songs by the end of last term.
A. had learned　　　B. learned
C. have learned　　　D. will have learned

( ) 33. Mother _____ me a nice present on my next birthday.
A. will gives　　B. will give　　C. gives　　D. give

( ) 34. Li Ming said he _____ happy if Brian _____ to China next month.
A. as; come　　　　　B. was; would come
C. would be; came　　D. will be; come

( ) 35. Jenny said she _____ her holiday in China.
A. spent　　　　　　　B. would spent
C. was going to spent　D. would spend

( ) 36. —_____ you _____ free tomorrow?
—No. I _____ free the day after tomorrow.

		A. Are; going to; will	B. Are; going to be; will
		C. Are; going to; will be	D. Are; going to be; will be

( ) 37. Han Mei told me she _____ lunch, so she was very hungry.

      A. has had   B. hasn't have   C. have had   D. hadn't had

( ) 38. By the end of 1976, many buildings _____ built in the city.

      A. have been   B. have   C. had been   D. will

( ) 39. He said that it was at least ten years since I _____ a good drink.

      A. had enjoyed   B. was enjoying

      C. have enjoyed   D. have been enjoying

( ) 40. —What did your son say in the letter?

    —He told me that he _____ the Disney World the next day.

      A. will visit   B. has visited

      C. is going to visit   D. would visit

第十一节　动词语态

一、概述

动词语态是指特殊的动词形式，用以表示动作的主语和宾语之间的关系。英语的语态有两种：主动语态和被动语态。主动语态中主语是动作的执行者，被动语态中主语是动作的承受者。

They will build a new bridge over the river.（主动语态）

A new bridge will be built over the river.（被动语态）

汉语中常用"被""给""由""受"等词来表示被动，而英语则由 be + 及物动词的过去分词构成。

二、被动语态的形式

（一）常用时态的被动语态的构成

1. 被动语态的基本形式为 be + 及物动词的过去分词，即 be done。

2. 被动语态的时态、人称和数的变化主要体现在 be 的变化上，其形式与系动词 be 的变化形式完全一样。以 give 为例，列表如下（表12）：

表12　被动语态的构成

项目	一般	进行	完成
现在	am/is/are given	am/is/are being given	has/have been given
过去	was/were given	was/were being given	had been given
将来	shall/will be given	—	shall/will have been given
过去将来	should/would be given	—	should/would have been given

注：(1) 含情态动词的被动语态：情态动词 + be done。

(2) 被动语态没有将来进行时和过去将来进行时。

（二）被动语态的否定式

在 be 后加 not 再加过去分词构成。

Russian is not taught in our school.

我们学校不教俄语。

This letter was not written by Lucy.

这封信不是露西写的。

（三）被动语态的疑问式

把 be 提到主语之前，句尾加问号构成。

Were many trees planted on the hill yesterday?

昨天山上种了许多树吗？

What was it made of?

它是什么做的？

三、被动语态使用范围

谁做的动作不知道，说出谁做的没必要。

动作承受者需强调，用被动语态莫忘了。

Some stamps were stolen last week.

上星期有些邮票被偷了。

The PRC was founded on October 1, 1949.

中华人民共和国成立于 1949 年 10 月 1 日。

Football is played in most middle schools.

大多数中学都踢足球。

四、主动句不能改为被动句的情况

(1) 感官系动词一般用主动形式表示被动意义，如：feel, look, seem, taste, sound, remain 等。

（正）The food tastes delicious.

（误）The food is tasted delicious.

（正）The pop music sounds beautiful.

（误）The pop music is sounded beautiful.

(2) 谓语是及物动词，如：leave, enter, reach, suit, have, lack, own 等。

（正）He entered the room and got his book.

（误）The room was entered and his book was got.

（正）She had her hand burned.

（误）Her hand was had burned.

(3) 不及物动词没有被动语态，如：rise, happen, succeed, remain, lie 等。

（正）When we got to the top of the mountain, the sun had already risen.

（误）The sun had already been risen.

（正）After the earthquake, few houses remained.

（误）After the earthquake, few houses were remained.

（4）一些不及物动词短语没有被动语态，如：take place, break out, belong to, consist of, add up to 等。

（正）The fire broke out in the building.

（误）The fire was broke out in the capital building.

（5）宾语是反身代词、相互代词、同源宾语、不定式、v-ing 形式及抽象名词等，不能变为被动句子的主语。

I taught myself English. （误）Myself was taught English.

We love each other. （误）Each other is loved.

（6）有些动词既是及物动词又是不及物动词，当它们和 well, badly, easily 等副词连用时，表示主语的内在品质或性能，是不及物动词，用主动表示被动，这时不用被动语态，常见的有：write, read, clean, sell, wash, cook 等：

The cloth washes easily. 这布很好洗。

The new product sells well. 这款新产品很畅销。

The pen writes smoothly. 这支笔写字很流畅。

真题分析

1. —Mom, where is my model plane?
   —Oh, it _____ to Jenny yesterday.
   A. is lent   B. lends   C. was lent   D. lent

   分析：——妈妈，我的飞机模型在哪里？——哦，昨天借给了詹妮。因为句子的主语是 it，代指的是 my model plane，my model plane 与 lend 之间是被动关系。句子的时间状语是 yesterday，所以应该用一般过去时的被动语态，故选 C。

2. In the past, the poor man _____ for a long time every day.
   A. was made to work   B. was made work
   C. made to work   D. made work

   分析：过去，这个可怜的人每天都要工作很长一段时间。本题考查被动语态。由题干可知本句的主语 the poor man 是动作的承受者，所以应用被动语态，其结构为"be + 动词过去分词"，所以排除 C、D 选项；根据 In the past 可知时态应用一般过去时，主语为 the poor man，所以系动词 be 用 was；make 为使役动词，其过去分词为 made，用于被动语态时后面的 to 不能省略，因此排除 B 选项；故选 A。

3. Children should _____ to be honest from a young age.
   A. educate   B. be educated   C. punish   D. be punished

   分析：应该从小教育孩子们做老实人。Children 是 educate 的承受者，该用被动语态。故选 B。

4. I will go out to play with you as soon as my homework _____.

A. finishes B. is finished C. will be finished D. was finished

分析：我的作业一做完我就出去和你玩。时间状语从句中，若主句是一般将来时，从句用一般现在时代替一般将来时；本题中从句的主语是 my homework，是动作的承受者，用被动语态，故选 B。

5. Smart phones _____ by Huawei are getting more and more popular around the world.
A. made B. making C. to make D. making

分析：由华为制造的智能手机在全世界正在变得越来越受欢迎。根据句意可知 _____ by Huawei 作前面 phones 的定语，并且表示被动，所以用动词过去分词作名词定语，即 made，故选 A。

实战演练

( ) 1. The People's Republic of China _____ on October 1, 1949.
A. found B. was founded C. is founded D. was found

( ) 2. English _____ in Canada.
A. speaks B. are spoken C. is speaking D. is spoken

( ) 3. This English song _____ by the girls after class.
A. often sings B. often sang C. is often sang D. is often sung

( ) 4. The key _____ on the table when I leave.
A. was left B. will be left C. is left D. has been left

( ) 5. New computers _____ all over the world.
A. is used B. are using C. are used D. have used

( ) 6. Our room must _____ clean.
A. keep B. be kept C. to be kept D. to keep

( ) 7. A new house _____ at the corner of the road.
A. is building B. is being built C. been built D. be building

( ) 8. His new book _____ next month.
A. will be published B. is publishing
C. is being published D. has been published

( ) 9. Lucy: My shoes are worn out.
Lily: _____
A. Can't they be mended? B. Can't they be mend?
C. Can't they mended? D. Can't they be mending?

( ) 10. Doctors _____ in every part of the world.
A. need B. are needing C. are needed D. will need

( ) 11. The flowers _____ often.
A. must be water B. must be watered
C. must watered D. must water

( ) 12. The boy _____ streets without pay in the old days.
A. was made to clean B. made clean

C. made to clean   D. was made clean

(   ) 13. The broken bike _____ here by Mr. Smith.
A. can mend   B. can mended
C. can be mend   D. can be mended

(   ) 14. The old bridge in my hometown _____ next month.
A. is going to be rebuilt   B. will rebuilt
C. are going to be rebuilt   D. are going to rebuild

(   ) 15. Great changes _____ in our country in the past 20 years.
A. have happened   B. happened
C. have been happened   D. were happened

(   ) 16. _____ the watch been repaired yet? I badly need it.
A. Does   B. Has   C. Is   D. Are

(   ) 17. _____ these desks be needed?
A. Will   B. Are   C. Has   D. Do

(   ) 18. I _____ in summer.
A. born   B. was born   C. have been born   D. am born

(   ) 19. Who was the book _____ ?
A. write   B. wrote   C. written   D. written by

(   ) 20. Where _____ these boxes made?
A. was   B. were   C. is   D. am

第十二节　非谓语动词

非谓语动词，又叫非限定动词，是指在句子中不是谓语的动词，主要包括不定式、分词（现在分词和过去分词）和动名词，即动词的非谓语形式。非谓语动词除了不能独立作谓语外，可以承担句子的其他成分。

一、动词不定式

（一）动词不定式的构成

(to) + do，具有名词、形容词、副词的特征，否定式：not + (to) do。以 do 为例，动词不定式的构成如下：

1. 一般式：不定式的一般式所表示的动作与谓语动词动作同时发生或发生在谓语动词动作之后。如：

It's nice to meet you.
很高兴见到你。

He seems to know a lot.
他看起来懂得很多。

We plan to pay a visit.
我们计划去参观。

He wants to be an artist.

他想成为一个艺术家。

The patient asked to be operated on at once.

病人要求马上手术。

The teacher ordered the work to be done.

老师要求完成工作。

2. 进行式：不定式的进行式所表示的动作与谓语动词动作同时发生。如：

The boy pretended to be working hard.

男孩假装工作得很努力。

He seems to be reading in his room.

看起来他正在他的房间里面读书。

3. 完成式：不定式的完成式表示的动作发生在谓语动词动作之前。如：

I happened to have seen the film.

我偶然看过这部电影。

He is pleased to have met his friend.

他很高兴能遇上他的朋友。

（二）不定式的句法功能

1. 作主语。

To finish the work in ten minutes is very hard.

10 分钟之内完成这项工作是很难的。

To lose your heart means failure.

灰心意味着失败。

动词不定式短语作主语时，常用 it 作形式主语，真正的主语不定式置于句后，例如上面两句可用如下形式：

It is very hard to finish the work in ten minutes.

10 分钟之内完成这项工作是很难的。

It means failure to lose your heart.

灰心意味着失败。

常用句式有：

（1）It + be + 名词 + to do。

（2）It takes sb. + some time + to do。

（3）It + be + 形容词 + of sb. + to do。常用 careless, clever, good, foolish, honest, kind, lazy, nice, right, silly, stupid, wise 等表示赞扬或批评的形容词，不定式前的 sb. 可作其逻辑主语。

2. 作表语。

Her job is to clean the hall.

她的工作是打扫大厅。

He appears to have caught a cold.

他似乎感冒了。

3. 作宾语。

常与不定式作宾语连用的动词有：begin，start，want，forget，remember，show，learn，like，hate，love，ask 等。

I want to tell you a story.

我想给你讲个故事。

They begin to work at eight every morning.

他们每天早晨8点开始工作。

Don't forget to lock the door.

别忘了锁门。

Would you like to go and have a picnic with us tomorrow?

明天和我们一起去野餐好吗？

如果 and 连接两个动词不定式，第二个动词不定式一般省"to"，如：

（1）He wants to go and have a swim with us.

他想和我们一起去游泳。

（2）若作宾语的动词不定式（短语）很长，可用 it 作形式宾语。

I find it interesting to learn English with you.

我觉得和你一起学英语很有趣。

He found it hard to catch up with others.

他觉得赶上别人很困难。

4. 作宾语补足语。

在复合宾语中，动词不定式可充当宾语补足语，以下动词常跟这种复合宾语：tell，ask，want，like，invite，encourage，help 等。

The teacher often tells Jim not to spend too much time playing computer games.

老师常告诉吉姆不要花太多时间玩电脑游戏。

The teacher asked us to read English for half an hour in the morning.

老师让我们早晨读半小时英语。

I want you to go now.

我想让你现在就走。

Her parents wish her to be a teacher.

她父母亲希望她当老师。

有些动词如 make，let，see，watch，hear，feel，have 等与不带有 to 的不定式连用，但改为被动语态时，不定式要加 to，如：

I saw him cross the road.

我看见他横过公路。

He was seen to cross the road.

他被我看见横过公路。

5. 作定语。

动词不定式作定语常用来修饰名词或不定代词，放于所修饰的词后，为后置定语。

Who was the first one to arrive?

谁第一个到的?

She has no paper to write on.

她没有纸写字。

The best way to learn English is to use it.

学英语最好的方法是使用它。

When is the best time to plant vegetables?

什么时候是种植蔬菜的最好时间?

Do you have something to drink? 你这有喝的吗?

如果不定式中的动词为不及物动词时,其后应加上一个含义上所需要的介词。

I have no chair to sit on.

我没有椅子坐。

He has no house to live in.

他没有房子住。

6. 作状语。

(1) 表目的。

He worked day and night to get the money.

他夜以继日地工作来赚钱。

She sold her hair to buy the watch chain.

她卖掉了自己的头发来买那条表链。

(2) 表结果(往往是与预期愿望相反的结果意料之外):常放在 never, only 后。

He arrived late only to find the train had gone.

他来晚了,只见火车已经走了。

I visited him only to find him out.

我去拜访他,只见他出去了。

(3) 表原因:常放在形容词后面。

They were very sad to hear the news.

他们听到这条新闻非常伤心。

(4) 表程度。

It's too dark for us to see anything.

太暗了,我们什么也看不见。

The question is simple for him to answer.

这问题由他来回答是很简单的。

二、现在分词

1. 现在分词既具有动词的一些特征,又具有形容词和副词的句法功能。

2. 现在分词的变化规则:

(1) 一般情况下,直接在动词后加-ing。

work—working

sleep—sleeping

study—studying

go—going

play—playing

know—knowing

walk—walking

eat—eating

beat—beating

sing—singing

（2）动词以不发音的-e结尾，要去-e加-ing。

take—taking

make—making

dance—dancing

write—writing

arrive—arriving

come—coming

（3）以重读闭音节结尾，且词尾只有一个辅音字母时，先双写这个辅音字母，再加-ing（重闭单辅先双写）。

cut—cutting

put—putting

begin—beginning

run—running

stop—stopping

prefer—preferring

（4）以-ie结尾，先将-ie改成y，再加-ing。

lie—lying

tie—tying

die—dying

3. 现在分词的形式：v-ing，否定式：not + v-ing。

（1）现在分词的主动语态：现在分词主动语态的一般式表示与谓语动词所表示的动作同时发生，完成式表示的动作在谓语动词所表示的动作之前发生，常作状语。例如：

They went to the park, singing and talking.

他们边唱边说向公园走去。

Having done his homework, he played basketball.

做完作业，他开始打篮球。

（2）现在分词的被动语态：一般式表示与谓语动词同时发生的被动的动作，完成式表示发生在谓语动词之前的被动的动作。

The problem being discussed is very important.

正在被讨论的问题很重要。

Having been told many times, the naughty boy made the same mistake.

被告诉了好几遍,这个淘气的孩子又犯了同一个错误。

4. 现在分词的句法功能。

(1) 作定语。

现在分词作定语,当分词单独作定语时,放在所修饰的名词前;如果是分词短语作定语放在名词后。

In the following years he worked even harder.

在后来的几年中,他学习更努力了。

The man speaking to the teacher is our monitor's father.

正与老师谈话的那个人是我们班长的父亲。

现在分词作定语相当于一个定语从句的句法功能,如:in the following years 也可用 in the years that followed;the man speaking to the teacher 可改为 the man who is speaking to the teacher.

(2) 作表语。

The film being shown in the cinema is exciting.

正在这家电影院上演的电影很棒。

The present situation is inspiring.

当前的形势鼓舞人心。

be + doing 既可能表示现在进行时,也可能是现在分词作表语,它们的区别在于 be + doing 表示进行的动作,是进行时,而表示特征时是系动词 be 与现在分词构成系表结构。

(3) 作宾语补足语。

如下动词后可跟现在分词作宾语补足语:

see, watch, hear, feel, find, get, keep, notice, observe, listen to, look at, leave, catch 等。例如:

Can you hear her singing the song in the next room?

你能听见她在隔壁唱歌吗?

He kept the car waiting at the gate.

他让小汽车在门口等着。

(4) 作状语。

①作时间状语:

(While) Working in the factory, he was an advanced worker.

在工厂工作时,他是一名先进工人。

②作原因状语:

Being a League member, he is always helping others.

由于是共青团员,他经常帮助他人。

③作方式状语,表示伴随:

He stayed at home, cleaning and washing.

他待在家里,又擦又洗。

④作条件状语:

(If) Playing all day, you will waste your valuable time.

要是整天玩,你就会浪费宝贵的时间。
⑤作结果状语:
He dropped the glass, breaking it into pieces.
他把杯子掉了,结果摔得粉碎。
⑥作目的状语:
He went swimming the other day.
几天前他去游泳了。
⑦作让步状语:
Though raining heavily, it cleared up very soon.
虽然雨下得很大,但不久天就晴了。
⑧与逻辑主语构成独立主格:
I waiting for the bus, a bird fell on my head.
我等汽车时,一只鸟落到我头上。
All the tickets having been sold out, they went away disappointedly.
所有的票已经卖光了,他们失望地离开了。
Time permitting, we'll do another two exercises.
如果时间允许,我们将做另两个练习。
有时也可用with(without)+名词(代词宾格)+分词形式
With the lights burning, he fell asleep.
他点着灯睡着了。
⑨作独立成分:
Judging from (by) his appearance, he must be an actor.
从外表看,他一定是个演员。
Generally speaking, girls are more careful.
一般来说,女孩子更细心。

三、过去分词

1. 过去分词既具有动词的一些特征,又具有形容词和副词的句法功能,通常含有被动意义。

2. 过去分词的变化规则:
(1) 一般动词加-ed。
work—worked
visit—visited
(2) 以 e 结尾的动词加-d。
live—lived
agree—agreed
(3) 以"辅音字母+y"结尾的动词,将"y"变为"i",再加-ed。
study—studied
cry—cried

try—tried

fry—fried

（4）重读闭音节结尾，末尾只有一个辅音字母，先双写该辅音字母，再加-ed。

stop—stopped

drop—dropped

3. 过去分词的句法功能：

（1）作定语：

Our class went on an organized trip last Monday.

上周一我们班开展了一次有组织的旅行。

Those selected as committee members will attend the meeting.

当选为委员的人将出席这次会议。

（2）作表语：

The window is broken.

窗户破了。

They were frightened at the sad sight.

他们对眼前悲惨的景象感到很害怕。

注意：be + 过去分词，如果表示状态是系表结构，如果表示被动的动作是被动语态。区别：

The window is broken.（系表）

The window was broken by the boy.（被动）

有些过去分词是不及物动词构成的，不表示被动，只表示完成。如：

boiled water（开水）

fallen leaves（落叶）

newly arrived goods（新到的货）

the risen sun（升起的太阳）

the changed world（变了的世界）

（3）作宾语补足语：

I heard the song sung several times last week.

上周我听见这首歌被唱了好几次。

有时过去分词作 with 短语中的宾语补足语：

With the work done, they went out to play.

工作做完了，他们出去玩了。

（4）作状语：

Praised by the neighbors, he became the pride of his parents.

受到邻居们的表扬，他成为父母的骄傲。（表示原因）

Once seen, it can never be forgotten.

一旦它被看见，人们就忘不了。（表示时间）

Given more time, I'll be able to do it better.

如果给予更多的时间，我能做得更好。（表示条件）

Though told of the danger, he still risked his life to save the boy.

虽然被告之有危险，他仍然冒生命危险去救那个孩子。（表示让步）

四、动名词

1. 动名词既具有动词的一些特征，又具有名词的句法功能（表13）。

表 13 动名词

一般式（谓语动词同时发生）	doing	being done
完成式（谓语动词发生之前）	having done	having been done

2. 动名词的形式：v-ing

否定式：not + 动名词

（1）一般式。

Seeing is believing.

眼见为实。

（2）被动式。

He came to the party without being invited.

他未被邀请就来到了晚会。

（3）完成式。

We remembered having seen the film.

我们记得看过这部电影。

（4）完成被动式。

He forgot having been taken to Guangzhou when he was five years old.

他忘记五岁时曾被带去过广州。

（5）否定式：not + 动名词。

I regret not following his advice.

我后悔没听他的劝告。

（6）复合结构：物主代词（或名词所有格）+ 动名词。

He suggested our trying it once again.

他建议我们再试一次。

His not knowing English troubled him a lot.

他不懂英语给他带来许多麻烦。

3. 动名词的句法功能：

（1）作主语。

Reading aloud is very helpful.

朗读是很有好处的。

Collecting stamps is interesting.

集邮很有趣。

（2）作表语。

In the ant city, the queen's job is laying eggs.

在蚂蚁王国，蚁后的工作是产卵。

（3）作宾语。

They haven't finished building the dam.

他们还没有建好大坝。

We have to prevent the air from being polluted.

我们必须阻止空气被污染。

注意动名词既可作动词宾语也可作介词宾语，如上面两个例句。此外，动名词作动词宾语时，若跟有宾语补足语，则常用形式宾语 it，例如：

We found it no good making fun of others.

我们发现取笑他人不好。

（4）作定语：

He can't walk without a walking – stick.

他没有拐杖不能走路。

Is there a swimming pool in your school?

你们学校有游泳池吗？

（5）作同位语：

The cave, his hiding-place is secret.

那个山洞，他藏身的地方很秘密。

His habit, listening to the news on the radio remains unchanged.

他收听收音机新闻节目的习惯仍未改变。

真题分析

1. I look forward _____ you soon.
   A. see　　　　　　B. seeing　　　　　　C. to see　　　　　　D. to seeing
   分析：我盼望尽快见到你。look forward to doing sth. 盼望做某事，故选 D。

2. Our teacher often tells us _____ in the river.
   A. not swim　　　　B. not to swim　　　　C. to swim　　　　D. swimming
   分析：题目中的 tell（告诉）是谓语，句子在连接第二个动词时，需要用 to 来连接，将其非谓语化，to + 动词原形，可以排除 A 和 D。可以推断出老师是告诉我们不要去游泳，因此选择不定式的否定形式，故选 B。

3. Fred hopes _____ his spoken English.
   A. improve　　　　B. improves　　　　C. improving　　　　D. to improve
   分析：弗雷德希望提高他的英语口语。hope to do，固定搭配，希望做，故此处是不定式，故选 D。

4. Please keep _____ and never give up.
   A. try　　　　　　B. tried　　　　　　C. trying　　　　　　D. to try
   分析：请坚持尝试，不要放弃。keep doing sth. 坚持做某事，固定短语，故选 C。

5. The winner is a boy _____ Lin Feng from Class 4.
   A. calls　　　　　　B. calling　　　　　　C. called　　　　　　D. to call

分析：获奖者是来自4班的叫林峰的男孩。分词短语作后置定语，ed 形式表示被动意义，ing 形式表示主动意义。结合语境可知应选 C。

实战演练

( ) 1. The story is _____. So we are _____ in it.
　　A. interest, interesting　　　　B. interesting, interesting
　　C. interested, interesting　　　D. interesting, interested

( ) 2. I'd like _____ a word with you.
　　A. had　　B. having　　C. to have　　D. have

( ) 3. Can you finish _____ an elephant in two minutes?
　　A. draw　　B. to draw　　C. drew　　D. drawing

( ) 4. The doctor was busy _____ on the boy at that time.
　　A. operate　　B. operating　　C. to operated　　D. operated

( ) 5. They kept the fire _____ to keep them warm.
　　A. to burn　　B. burn　　C. burnt　　D. burning

( ) 6. Who's the boy _____ under the tree?
　　A. stand　　B. to stand　　C. standing　　D. stood

( ) 7. The girl students enjoy _____ English songs.
　　A. singing　　B. to sing　　C. sing　　D. sung

( ) 8. Thank you for _____ us so well.
　　A. to teach　　B. teaches　　C. teaching　　D. taught

( ) 9. I often do some _____ on Sundays.
　　A. washed　　B. to wash　　C. wash　　D. washing

( ) 10. The boy _____ Li Hua in Class One is his brother.
　　A. called　　B. calling　　C. to call　　D. call

( ) 11. It often takes me half an hour _____ home.
　　A. walking　　B. to walk　　C. walked　　D. walk

( ) 12. Don't forget _____ her clean water every day.
　　A. to give　　B. giving　　C. given　　D. give

( ) 13. I think it important _____ English well.
　　A. learning　　B. learn　　C. to learn　　D. learned

( ) 14. The funny story makes us _____.
　　A. laugh　　B. laughing　　C. to laugh　　D. laughed

( ) 15. She was often heard _____ in English.
　　A. sing　　B. singing　　C. sung　　D. to sing

( ) 16. Our teacher told us _____ hard.
　　A. to work　　B. working　　C. worked　　D. work

( ) 17. Could you tell me _____ this word?
　　A. to how read　　　　B. how to read

C. how read D. how read to

( ) 18. Remember _____ late for class again.
A. not to   B. not to be   C. to be not   D. be not to

( ) 19. Stop _____, please. I've something to tell you.
A. to read   B. reading   C. read   D. to write

( ) 20. Please tell him _____ the light when he leaves.
A. to turn off   B. turn down
C. turn off   D. to turn down

第十三节　句子的基本句型

一、概述

句子是一个语言单位。它是由单词按照一定的语法结构和语法规则构成的，并表达一个完整而独立的意思。句子的首字母必须大写，句子的末尾则有句号、问号或感叹号。

英语句子的基本成分有七种：主语（subject）、谓语（predicate）、宾语（object）、表语（predicative）、补语（complement）、定语（attribute）和状语（adverbial）。

二、英语句子的基本句型

英语句子的五种基本句型如下：
基本句型一：　　S + V　　　　　　　　　（主 + 谓）
基本句型二：　　S + V + O　　　　　　　（主 + 谓 + 宾）
基本句型三：　　S + V + P　　　　　　　（主 + 系 + 表）
基本句型四：　　S + V + indirectO + directO　（主 + 谓 + 间宾 + 直宾）
基本句型五：　　S + V + O + C　　　　　（主 + 谓 + 宾 + 宾补）

基本句型一

此句型中的谓语动词都能够表达完整的意思，这类动词叫作不及物动词，后面可以跟副词、介词短语、状语从句等。

S + V（不及物动词）

1. A new semester　　　　| begins in September.
2. The sun　　　　　　　| rises in the east every morning.
3. We　　　　　　　　　| breathe, eat and drink every day.
4. Jack and Frank　　　　| get up early every morning.
5. The rain　　　　　　　| has stopped.
6. What she said　　　　　| does not matter.
7. His brother　　　　　　| has worked in the factory for more than ten years.

基本句型二

此句型中的谓语动词都具有实际意义，都是主语执行的动作，但不能表达完整的意思，必须跟有一个宾语（动作的承受者），才能使句子的意思完整，这类动词叫作及物动词。

S + V（及物动词）+ O

1. I	often do	some part-time jobs.
2. Who	knows	the answer?
3. They	ate	what was left over.
4. Tom	opened	the door.
5. You	may ask	any questions you have during the visit.
6. He	admits	that he was mistaken.
7. They	favor	the idea that the college life is comfortable.

基本句型三

此句型中的谓语动词不能表达一个完整的意思，必须加上一个表明主语身份或状态的表语，这类动词叫作连系动词或系动词。系动词有两类：be, look, keep, seem（表示情况）；get, grow, become, turn（表示变化）。be 本身并没有什么意义，只起联系主语和表语的作用，其他系动词仍保持其部分词义。

S + V（连系动词）+ P

1. This	is	an French-Chinese dictionary.
2. The flower	smells	sweet.
3. He	fell	in love with a beautiful girl.
4. Everything	looks	different.
5. The reason	is	that they are short of money.
6. The well	has gone	dry.
7. His face	turned	red.

基本句型四

此句型中的谓语动词必须跟有两个宾语才能表达完整的意思。这两个宾语一个是动作的间接承受者，一般指人，叫间接宾语（indirect object），另一个是动作的直接承受者，一般指物，叫直接宾语（direct object）。有时，间接宾语也可改为由介词 to 或 for 引起的短语，放在直接宾语的后面。常跟双宾语的动词有 give, show, bring, pass, lend, tell, leave, teach, write, buy, sing 等。

S + V（及物动词）+ indirectO（间宾）+ directO（直宾）

1. The man	gave	Tom	a piece of paper.
2. He	showed	us	a new TV set.
3. She	brought	you	a dictionary.
4. He	passed	him	the salt.
5. Grandma	bought	her	a nice present.
6. They	teach	the foreigners	Chinese.
7. I	told	him	that the bus was late.

基本句型五

此句型中的动词虽然是及物动词，但是只跟一个宾语还不能表达完整的意思，必须加上宾语补足语来补充说明宾语的有关情况，才能使意思完整。宾语和宾语补足语合称复合宾语。一些动词后面常跟复合宾语，这类动词有 let, see, watch, hear, help, keep, call, make, find, tell, ask, think, want 等。宾语和宾语补足语之间关系比较紧密，去掉其中一个成分，句子就不能成立或句意不完整。当名词、形容词、副词、介词短语作宾语补足语时，宾语和宾语补足语之间具有"主系表关系"；当不定式（短语）或分词（短语）作宾语补足语时，宾语和宾语补足语之间具有"主谓关系"。

S + V（及物动词）+ O（宾语）+ C（宾补）

1. We	will make	our country	more beautiful.
2. His parents	named	her	Alice.
3. They	appointed	him	general manager.
4. We	must keep	the classroom	clean.
5. I	found	the boy	in Room 201.
6. She	helps	her mother	do some housework.
7. We	heard	her	singing in the room.

在句子中词类和词的位置也影响句子的句型和意思：

I found the book easily.
我很容易地找到了这本书。

I found the book easy.
我觉得这本书很容易。

真题分析

1. The cheese cake _____ so good.
   A. taste　　　B. feels　　　C. sounds　　　D. smells
   分析：奶酪蛋糕闻起来这么香。taste 品尝；feel 感觉；sound 听起来；smell 闻起来。这四个词都是系动词，后跟形容词作表语，故选 D。

2. The weather is _____.
   A. bad　　　B. badly　　　C. well　　　D. worse
   分析：考查表语的句子成分。句意：天气很糟（好）。形容天气，表语应该为形容词原形，故选 A。

3. My friend show _____ some old photos of his family.
   A. my　　　B. I　　　C. me　　　D. mine
   分析：考查宾语成分。动词之后缺宾语，排除 B 和 D；又根据句意，朋友给我展现，故选 C。

4. Please keep the classroom _____ when you left.
   A. clean　　　B. cleanly　　　C. cleaning　　　D. clear
   分析：离开时请保持教室清洁。缺少宾语补足语，应为形容词，排除 B 和 C；A. 干净的；D. 清楚的，故选 A。

5. He got up _____ yesterday morning.
   A. lately　　　　　B. late　　　　　　C. latest　　　　　D. latter

分析：考查状语成分。根据句意：他昨天早上很晚起床，缺少修饰起床的状语，A. 最近；B. 晚，迟；C. 最新的；D. 后来，故选 B。

实战演练

( ) 1. The earth _____ round the sun.
　　　A. move　　　B. moves　　　　　C. moved　　　　　D. will move

( ) 2. Mr. Smith _____ here since he came to China three years ago.
　　　A. has lived　　B. have lived　　　C. had lived　　　　D. have live

( ) 3. He got up _____ yesterday morning.
　　　A. lately　　　B. late　　　　　　C. latest　　　　　D. latter

( ) 4. Hardly _____ at the office when the telephone rang.
　　　A. I arrived　　　　　　　　　　　B. I had arrived
　　　C. had I arrived　　　　　　　　　D. did I arrive

( ) 5. I've lost my watch. _____ you seen it anywhere?
　　　A. Have　　　B. Had　　　　　　C. Has　　　　　　D. Having

( ) 6. She likes watering trees in the garden, _____ she?
　　　A. didn't　　　B. don't　　　　　C. isn't　　　　　　D. doesn't

( ) 7. He said he _____ the Party for two years.
　　　A. has joined　　　　　　　　　　B. had been in
　　　C. has been in　　　　　　　　　　D. joined

( ) 8. Taiwan Region is _____ the southeast of China.
　　　A. to　　　　　B. on　　　　　　C. in　　　　　　　D. of

( ) 9. The dog _____ mad.
　　　A. looks　　　B. is looked　　　　C. is being looked　D. was looked

( ) 10. Roses in bloom smell _____.
　　　A. sweeten　　B. sweetly　　　　C. sweet　　　　　D. sweetness

( ) 11. She teaches Chinese _____ the foreigners in her spare time.
　　　A. at　　　　　B. for　　　　　　C. to　　　　　　　D. on

( ) 12. They asked him to sing _____ an English song.
　　　A. them　　　B. they　　　　　　C. their　　　　　　D. theirs

( ) 13. I told Tom _____ the TV since it was too late.
　　　A. turn off　　B. turns off　　　　C. to turn off　　　　D. turning off

( ) 14. They ordered her to remove her veil, but she _____.
　　　A. refused　　B. refuses　　　　　C. did refusal　　　　D. refusal

( ) 15. I am sorry to have kept you _____.
　　　A. to wait　　　B. wait　　　　　　C. waited　　　　　D. waiting

(　) 16. No student is allowed _____ any reference books out of the reading-room.
　　　A. to take　　B. taking　　　　　C. take　　　　　　D. took

(　) 17. They knew her very well. They had seen her _____ up from childhood.
　　　A. was growing　　　　　　　　B. grew
　　　C. grow　　　　　　　　　　　　D. to grow

(　) 18. He told _____ home.
　　　A. us not to go　　　　　　　　B. we not go
　　　C. us not go　　　　　　　　　　D. us to not go

(　) 19. I found him _____ on the floor.
　　　A. lie　　　B. lain　　　　　　　C. lied　　　　　　　D. lying

(　) 20. I think _____ a good habit to get up early.
　　　A. this　　　B. it　　　　　　　　C. that　　　　　　　D. its

第十四节　状语从句

在复合句中作状语的从句叫状语从句。状语从句一般由连词（从属连词）引导，也可以由词组引导。根据其作用状语从句可分为九种：时间状语从句、地点状语从句、条件状语从句、原因状语从句、目的状语从句、结果状语从句、让步状语从句、方式状语从句、比较状语从句。

一、时间状语从句

1. 概述。

时间状语从句指用来表示时间，修饰主句的从句。

2. 构成。

连接时间状语从句的连接词有：when, before, after, while, as soon as, until, since…在复合句中，要注意主句和从句的时态大多都要保持一致。如果主句是一般将来时，从句只能用一般现在时表示将来意义。

3. 引导时间状语从句连词的用法。

（1）when, while。

when 引导的时间状语从句，常译为"当……的时候"，when 从句既可用短暂性动词，也可用延续性动词；既可用点时间，也可用段时间。

He was working at the table when I went in.

当我进去的时候，他正在桌旁工作。

Someone knocked at the door when I was sleeping.

当我正在睡觉时，有人敲门。

while 引导的时间状语从句，常译为"与……同时，在……期间"，while 的从句中常用延续性动词或表示状态的词。

Strike while the iron is hot.

趁热打铁。

They broke in while we were discussing problems.

当我们正在讨论问题时，他们冲了进来。

（2）as。

as 引导的时间状语从句，常译为"当……的时候，一边……一边……"，as 引导的动作是延续性的动作，一般表示主句和从句动作同时发生。

He sang as he was working.

他一边工作一边唱歌。

As we was going out, it began to snow.

当我们出门时，开始下雪了。（as 强调句中两个动作紧接着先后发生，而不强调开始下雪的特定时间）

（3）before, after。

由 before 和 after 引导的时间状语从句。注意 before 引导的从句不再用否定式的谓语，并且当 before 引导的从句位于主句之后，有时译成"就，才"。After 表示主句动作发生在从句动作之后，指主句和从句的动作的时间关系正好与 before 引导的从句相反。例如：

It will be four days before they come back.

他们要过四天才能回来。

Look before you leap.

三思而后行。

After you think it over, please let me know what you decide.

你仔细考虑过以后，告诉我你是怎样决定的。

After we had finished the work, we went home.

完成工作之后，我们回家了。（从句用过去完成时，主句用一般过去时）

（4）till, until。

由 till 或 until 引导的时间状语从句。till 和 until 一般情况下两者可以互换，但是在强调句型中多用 until。并且要注意的是：如果主句中的谓语动词是短暂性动词时，必须用否定形式；构成 not...until 结构，译为"直到……才"或"在……之前不"。

Not until you told media I have any idea of it.

直到你告诉媒体我知道了。

He didn't leave there until she arrived.

直到她到达他才离开那里。

He remained there until she arrived.

他一直待在那里直到她到达。

（5）since。

由 since 引导的时间状语从句。since 引导的从句的谓语动词可以是延续性动词，也可以是短暂性动词。一般情况下，从句谓语动词用一般过去时，而主句的谓语动词用现在完成时。

I have been in Beijing since you left.

自从你离开以来，我一直在北京。

Where have you been since I last saw you?

自上次我和你见面以后,你到哪里去了?

(6) as soon as。

由 as soon as 引导的时间状语从句,表示"一……就"。例如:

As soon as I reach Canada, I will ring you up.

我一到加拿大,就给你来电话。

一般情况下,时间和条件状语从句的谓语动词用"一般现在时"表示"一般将来时",用"现在完成时"表示"将来完成时"。

I will call you as soon as I arrive in Beijing.

我到北京就将给你打电话。(这是由 as soon as 引导的时间状语从句,从句中的谓语动词 arrive 是一般现在时,表示一般将来时,绝不可用 will arrive)

As soon as I have finished this work, I will have gone home.

我一完成此工作,就回家。(从句中的谓语动词用现在完成时 have finished,表示将来完成时,绝不可用 will have finished)

二、地点状语从句

1. 概述。

表示地点、方位的状语从句叫地点状语从句。

2. 构成。

地点状语从句由 where,wherever 引导。

3. 用法。

Where I live there are plenty of trees.

我住的地方树很多。

Wherever I am , I will be thinking of you.

不管我在哪里,我都会想到你。

三、条件状语从句

1. 概述。

由引导词 if 或 unless 引导的状语从句叫条件状语从句。在英文中,条件是指某一件事情实现之后(状语从句中的动作),其他事情(主句中的动作)才能发生,通常译作"假如"。

2. 构成。

引导条件状语从句的连词有:if(如果),unless(除非;如果不),as long as(除非;只要)。

3. 用法。

(1) if。

引导条件状语从句最常用的连词是 if,由 if 引导的条件状语从句表示在某种条件下某事很可能发生。

If you ask him, he will help you.

如果你请他帮忙,他会帮你的。

If you fail in the exam, you will let him down.
如果你考试不及格,你会让他失望的。

另外,if从句还表示不可实现的条件或根本不可能存在的条件,也就是一种虚拟的条件或假设,从句多用一般过去时或过去完成时。如:

If I were you, I would invite him to the party.
如果我是你,我会邀请他参加聚会。

I would have arrived much earlier if I had not been caught in the traffic.
如果没有堵车,我会到得早一点儿。

(2) unless。

unless 除非,若不,除非在……的时候

You will fail to arrive there in time unless you start earlier.
如果你不早点动身,你就不能及时赶到那儿。

Unless it rains, the game will be played.
除非下雨,比赛将照常进行。

(3) as long as。

as/so long as 只要

You may borrow my book as long as you keep it clean.
只要你保持书的清洁,你就可以把我的书借去。

So long as you're happy, it doesn't matter what you do.
只要你高兴,你做什么都没有关系。

四、原因状语从句

1. 概述。

表示原因的状语从句叫原因状语从句。

2. 构成。

常用的引导原因状语从句的连词有:because, as, since, for。

3. 用法。

(1) because。

because引导的原因状语从句一般放于主句之后,because表示直接原因,语气最强,最适合回答why引导的疑问句。例如:

I didn't buy it because it was too expensive.
我没有买是因为它太贵了。

She didn't go because she was afraid.
她没有去是因为怕。

注意:"not...because"结构中的not否定的是because引导的整个从句,例如:

The country is not strong because it is large.
国强不在大。

(2) since。

since引导的原因状语从句一般放于主句之前表示已知的、显然的理由(通常被翻译成

"既然"），较为正式，语气比 because 弱。例如：
　　Since you are free today, you had better help me with my mathematics.
　　既然今天你休息，你最好帮我补习数学。
　　Since it is so hot, let's go swimming.
　　既然天气这么热，我们去游泳吧。
　　(3) as。
　　as 引导原因状语从句时表示附带说明的"双方已知的原因"，语气比 since 弱，较为正式，位置较为灵活（常放于主句之前）。例如：
　　As it is raining, you'd better take a taxi.
　　既然在下雨，你最好乘出租汽车。
　　As you are tired, you had better rest.
　　既然累了，你最好休息一下。
　　I went to bed early, as I was exhausted.
　　我睡得早，因为我筋疲力尽了。
　　(4) for。
　　for 引导的是并列句表示原因但并不说明主句行为发生的直接原因，只提供一些辅助性的补充说明，for 引导的并列句只能放于主句之后并且必须用逗号将其与主句隔开。例如：
　　He could not have seen me, for I was not there.
　　他不可能见过我，因为我不在那里。

五、目的状语从句

1. 概述。
目的状语从句是用以补充说明主句中谓语动词发生的目的的句子。
2. 构成。
引导词：that（以便），so that（以便），in order that（为了；以便），lest（免得；唯恐），for fear that（生怕；以免）等。
目的状语从句的谓语常含有 may, might, can, could, should, would 等情态动词。
3. 用法。
　　You must speak louder so that/in order that you can be heard by all.
　　你必须说话大声点，以便别人可以听到你说话。
　　He wrote the name down for fear that (lest) he should forget it.
　　他把名字写下来以免忘记。
　　Better take more clothes in case the weather is cold.
　　最好多带些衣服以防天气会冷。
　　Say it louder (so) that everyone can hear you.
　　大声说，以便大家都能听到你。
　　I am telling you that lest you should make a mistake.
　　我告诉你这一点，以免你搞错。
　　Speak clearly, so that they may understand.

你必须说清楚点，以便别人可以明白你的意思。

She has bought the book in order that she could follow the lessons.

＝She has bought the book in order to follow the lessons.

她买了这本书，以便她可以跟得上课程。

六、结果状语从句

1. 概述。

结果状语从句是表示事情结果的句子，通常主句表示原因，从句表示结果。

2. 构成。

引导词：so that，so…that，such…that 等。结果状语从句表示事情的结果，通常位于主句之后。

3. 用法。

（1）so that 可以引导目的状语从句，也可以引导结果状语从句。

I came to the class early so that I could see the classmate beside me.

我赶早来上课，以便早点看到我旁边的同学。（so that 引导目的状语从句）

He worried so that he couldn't sleep.

他急得睡不着觉。（so that 引导结果状语从句）

It was very cold so that the river froze.

天气寒冷，河水都结冰了。（so that 引导结果状语从句）

（2）表示"如此……以至于……"的"so…that…"和"such…that…"都可以引导结果状语从句，其中 so 是副词，修饰形容词或副词；such 是形容词，修饰名词。具体搭配形式如下：

①so + adj./adv. + that。

Some people were so moved by the sight that they began to cry.

一些人对此情景如此感动，以致开始哭了出来。

He speaks so fast that no one can catch him.

他说话太快，无人听得明白。

②so + adj.（+ a/an）+ n. + that。

It was so hot a day that they wanted to go swimming.

天那么热，他们想去游泳。

Ada is so lovely a girl that all like her very much.

Ada 是如此可爱的一个女孩，结果是所有人都非常喜欢她。

③such（+ a/an）（+ adj.）+ n. + that。

He's such a good person that we mustn't blame him.

他是这样好的人，我们不能怪他。

He is such a clever boy that everybody likes him.

他非常聪明，大家都非常喜欢他。

④such（+ adj.）+ 复数名词 + that。

They are such clever children that his teachers all like them.

他们是如此聪明的孩子,老师都喜欢他们。
They are such interesting novels that I want to read them once again.
这些小说非常有趣,我想再读一遍。
⑤such (+adj.)+不可数名词+that。
It was such bad weather that they had to stay in the airport all day.
天气是如此的糟糕,结果是他们不得不一整天都留在机场。
He has made such great progress that the teachers are pleased with him.
他进步得很快,老师们对他感到很满意。
⑥so+many/much/few/little+adj.+n+that。
There are so many picture-story books that the boy won't leave.
有那么多连环画书,小孩都不想离开了。
There was so much homework to do that Tom got tired.
有太多的作业要做,结果是Tom太累。
I ate such few in the morning that I was very hungry now.
我早上吃得太少,现在非常饿。
He gave me so little time that it was impossible for me to finish the work on time.
他给我的时间如此少,要我按时完成任务是不可能的。

七、让步状语从句

1. 概述。
让步状语从句一般翻译为"尽管……即使……",就是我们日常生活中用的"退一步说……"的感觉。
2. 构成。
引导词:though, although, as; even if, even though; whether...or...; no matter+疑问词,疑问词-ever 等。
3. 用法。
(1) though, although 表示"虽然,纵然"之意。
这两个连词意思大致相同,在一般情况下可以互换使用。在口语中,though 较常使用,although 比 though 正式,二者都可与 yet, still 或 nevertheless 连用,但不能与 but 连用。
Although/Though he was worn out, (still) he kept on working.
虽然他已经精疲力竭了,但仍然继续工作。
Although/Though he is very old, (yet) he is quite strong.
他虽然年纪大了,身体还很健壮。
(2) as, though 表示"虽然……但是""纵使……"之意。
as 引导的让步状语从句必须以部分倒装的形式出现,被倒装的部分可以是表语、状语或动词原形,though 间或也用于这样的结构中,但 although 不可以这样用。
Hard as/though he works, he makes little progress.
=Though he works hard, he makes little progress.
尽管他学习很努力,但几乎没取得什么进步。

Child as/though he was, he knew what was the right thing to do.
= Though he was a child, he knew what was the right thing to do.
虽然他是一个孩子，但他知道该做什么。

（3）even if, even though 表示"即使……""纵使……"之意。

这两个复合连词的意思基本相同。它们常可互换使用，但意义有细微差别。even if 引导的让步状语从句含有强烈的假定性，而 even though 引导让步状语从句时，是以从句的内容为先决条件的，也就是说，说话人肯定了从句的事实。

We'll make a trip even if/though the weather is bad.
即使天气不好，我们也要作一次旅行。

Even if he is poor, she loves him.
= He may be poor, yet she loves him.
即使他很穷，但她还是爱他。

八、方式状语从句

1. 概述。
表示方式的状语从句叫方式状语从句，多用来谈论某人的行为或者做某事的方式。
2. 构成。
引导词：as, (just) as...so..., as if, as though 等。
3. 用法。

（1）as, (just) as...so...引导的方式状语从句通常位于主句后，但在 (just) as...so...结构中位于句首，这时 as 从句带有比喻的含义，意思是"正如""就像"，多用于正式文体。

You must try to hold the tool as I do.
你必须像我这样拿工具。

As water is to fish, so air is to man.
我们离不开空气，犹如鱼儿离不开水。

（2）as if, as though 两者的意义和用法相同，引出的状语从句谓语多用虚拟语气，表示与事实相反，有时也用陈述语气，表示所说情况是事实或实现的可能性较大。汉译常作"仿佛……似的""好像……似的"。

They completely ignore these facts as if (as though) they never existed.
他们完全忽略了这些事实，就仿佛它不存在似的。（与事实相反，谓语用虚拟语气。）

He looks as if (as though) he had been hit by lightning.
他那样子就像被雷击了似的。（与事实相反，谓语用虚拟语气。）

It looks as if the weather may pick up very soon.
看来天气很快就会好起来。（实现的可能性较大，谓语用陈述语气。）

说明：as if/as though 也可以引导一个分词短语、不定式短语或无动词短语。

He stared at me as if seeing me for the first time.
他目不转睛地看着我，就像第一次看见我似的。

He cleared his throat as if to say something.
他清了清嗓子，像要说什么似的。

九、比较状语从句

1. 概述。

比较状语从句主要运用于形容词和副词的原级、比较级及最高级的句子之中。

2. 构成。

（1）引导词。

原级：as...as（和……一样），not so（as）...as...（和……不一样）；

比较级：比较级＋than（更）；

最高级：The most...in/of, the＋形容词＋est...of/in。

（2）常用引导词：as（同级比较），than（不同程度的比较）。

（3）特殊引导词：the more...the more...；no...more than；not A so much as B。

3. 用法。

（1）as＋形容词/副词原级＋（名词）＋as...，"和……一样……"，否定句中副词 as 可以替换为 so。

He woke up as suddenly as he had fallen asleep.

他醒来得和入睡时一样突然。

He works as hard as his brother.

他和他哥哥一样努力学习。

（2）比较级＋than（更）。

The youth of today are better than we used to be.

如今的年轻人的境况比我们过去要好很多。

She did the job better than I thought.

这项工作她做得比我想象的要好。

（3）not so much...as... "与其说……不如说……"。

He is not so much a scholar as a businessman.

他与其说是个学者倒不如说是个商人。

（4）sb./sth. is more A than B "与其说 sb./sth. 是 B，不如说是 A"。

He is more an artist than a philosopher.

与其说他是位哲学家，不如说他是位艺术家。

（5）no more...than... "两者都不……"。

The heart is no more intelligent than the stomach, for they are both controlled by the brain.

心脏和胃一样都无智力可言，因为它们都是由大脑控制的。

（6）no more than... "只是，只不过，无非"。

Death is no more than passing from one room into another.

死亡只不过是从一个房间进入另一个房间。

（7）not more than... "不超过，至多"。

I have not more than two dollars left in my pocket.

我口袋里顶多还有两美元。

（8）no less than... "多达……，有……之多；简直，与……没差别"。

No less than nine of our agents have passed information to us.

多达 9 名特工向我们传递了情报。

（9）not less than… "不少于，至少"。

It is estimated that not less than half a million people died in the war.

据估计，死于这场战争的人数不少于 50 万。

（10）rather than… "而不是"。

These are political rather than social matters.

这是政治问题而不是社会问题。

（11）other than… "除了"。

no other than = none other than "正是"

He has no friends other than you.

他除你之外就没有别的朋友了。

This is no other than my old friend, John.

这位不是别人，正是我的老朋友约翰。

（12）the + 比较级，the + 比较级 "越……，越……"。

The more we can do for our country, the prouder we will feel.

为祖国做得越多我们就越感到自豪。

真题分析

1. She stopped talking _____ her mother came into the room.
   A. as soon as   B. unless   C. though   D. if

   分析：她妈妈一进到房间里，她就停止了说话。A. as soon as 一……就……；B. unless 除非；C. though 尽管；D. if 如果。根据 She stopped talking 和 her mother came into the room. 之间的关系，可知是妈妈一进到房间里，她就停止了说话；故选 A。

2. Chen Wei isn't at school today _____ he is taking a competition in Shanghai.
   A. so   B. because   C. before   D. if

   分析：陈炜今天不在学校因为他在上海参加比赛。so 所以；because 因为；before 在……之前；if 如果。所以选 B。

3. We didn't cut the cake _____ Amy made a wish.
   A. because   B. until   C. if   D. before

   分析：直到艾米许了愿，我们才切蛋糕。A. because 因为；B. until 直到；C. if 如果；D. before 在……之前。didn't 是 did not 的缩写。not until 直到……才。结合句意可知，答案为 B。

4. You will fall behind others _____ you work hard.
   A. if   B. unless   C. though   D. since

   分析：如果你不努力学习，你会落后别人。A. if 如果；B. unless 如果不；C. though 虽然；D. since 因为。结合句意，故选 B。

5. You'd better take the map with you _____ you won't get lost.
   A. so that   B. as soon as   C. now that   D. as long as

分析：你最好带上地图，这样你就不会迷路。A. 以便于，表目的；B. 一……就……，表条件；C. 既然，表原因；D. 只要，表条件。根据题干可知你最好带上地图的目的是不会迷路，本句是 so that 引导的目的状语从句，故选 A。

实战演练

( ) 1. _____ he is, he will be thinking of you.
  A. Wherever B. Where C. Now that D. As soon as

( ) 2. You should make it a rule to leave things _____ you can find them again.
  A. when B. where C. then D. there

( ) 3. —Shall Brown come and play computer games?
  —No, _____ he has finished his homework.
  A. when B. if C. unless D. once

( ) 4. _____ you try, you will never succeed.
  A. If B. Until C. Since D. Unless

( ) 5. —The air is full of smoke and people are coughing.
  —It will get worse _____ the government does something about the pollution.
  A. but B. unless C. except D. if

( ) 6. If _____, I would have gone with him.
  A. had he told me B. he had told me
  C. he has told me D. he would tell me

( ) 7. —Alice is moving to her new apartment next Saturday.
  —I'll be glad to help her, _____ need some help.
  A. should she B. if she will
  C. if she D. if she might

( ) 8. I came _____ I heard the news.
  A. until B. as soon as C. immediately D. B and C

( ) 9. _____ he comes, we would not be able to go.
  A. Without B. Unless C. Except D. Even

( ) 10. Telephone me as soon as you _____ the results.
  A. will get B. get C. had got D. got

( ) 11. _____ I live, I will never give in to the enemy.
  A. As far as B. As long as C. As well as D. As soon as

( ) 12. I was about to leave my house _____ the phone rang.
  A. while B. when C. as D. after

( ) 13. I had cut the meat into pieces _____ Mother started cooking.
  A. when B. as soon as C. after D. while

( ) 14. Babies sleep 16 to 18 hours in every 24 hours, and they sleep less _____ they grow older.
  A. while B. as C. when D. after

( ) 15. What a tight volleyball game! We lost it _____ we all tried our best.
　　　　A. though　　B. because　　　　C. until　　　　　D. unless

( ) 16. This is a very interesting book. I'll buy it , _____ .
　　　　A. how much may it cost　　　　B. no matter how it may cost
　　　　C. however much it may cost　　D. how may it cost

( ) 17. The reason why I burst into tears is _____ I don't want to part with my mother.
　　　　A. that　　　B. which　　　　C. /　　　　　　　D. because

( ) 18. _____ the professor had left, everyone looked relaxed.
　　　　A. While　　B. After　　　　C. Unless　　　　D. For

( ) 19. Her mother has been ill _____ she came to Beijing last year.
　　　　A. since　　　B. for　　　　　C. as　　　　　　D. when

( ) 20. I have taken care of your children _____ you were away.
　　　　A. for　　　　B. since　　　　C. except　　　　D. while

( ) 21. The lawyer seldom wears anything other than a suit _____ the season.
　　　　A. whatever　　B. wherever　　C. whenever　　　D. however

( ) 22. Many of them didn't listen to his advice, _____ they knew it to be valuable.
　　　　A. as if　　　B. now that　　　C. even though　　D. so that

( ) 23. _____ I really don't like art, I find his work impressive.
　　　　A. As　　　　B. Since　　　　C. If　　　　　　D. While

( ) 24. _____ he has limited technical knowledge, the old worker has a lot of experience.
　　　　A. Since　　　B. Unless　　　　C. As　　　　　　D. Although

( ) 25. _____ I have some sympathy for them, I don't think they are right to do so.
　　　　A. As　　　　B. If　　　　　　C. While　　　　D. When

( ) 26. _____ the Customs Office, he will have to declare this sort of things he carries with him to the Customs Officer.
　　　　A. No matter who will come through　　B. who come through
　　　　C. No matter whom comes through　　　D. Whoever comes through

( ) 27. The little boy won't go to sleep _____ his mother tells him a story.
　　　　A. or　　　　B. unless　　　　C. but　　　　　D. whether

( ) 28. We _____ Beijing tomorrow if it doesn't rain.
　　　　A. are going　B. would go　　　C. shall go　　　D. will go to

( ) 29. All people, _____ they are old or young, rich or poor, have been trying their best to help those in need since the disaster.
　　　　A. even if　　B. whether　　　C. no matter　　　D. however

( ) 30. Allow children the space to voice their opinions, _____ they are different from your own.
　　　　A. until　　　B. even if　　　C. unless　　　　D. as though

( ) 31. Several weeks had gone by _____ I realized the painting was missing.
　　　　A. as　　　　B. before　　　　C. since　　　　　D. when

( ) 32. It _____ long before we _____ the result of the experiment.
   A. will not be; will know   B. is; will know
   C. will not be; know   D. is; know

( ) 33. —What was the party like?
   —Wonderful. It's years _____ I enjoyed myself so much.
   A. after   B. before   C. when   D. since

( ) 34. The new secretary is supposed to report to the manager as soon as she _____.
   A. will arrive   B. arrives   C. is going to arrive   D. is arriving

( ) 35. _____ got into the room _____ the telephone rang.
   A. He hardly had; then   B. Hardly had he; when
   C. He had not; then   D. Not had he; when

( ) 36. No sooner had he finished his talk _____ he was surrounded by the workers.
   A. as   B. then   C. than   D. when

( ) 37. —Did you remember to give Mary the money you owed her?
   —Yes, I gave it to her _____ I saw her.
   A. while   B. the moment   C. suddenly   D. once

( ) 38. I thought her nice and honest _____ I met her.
   A. first time   B. for the first time
   C. the first time   D. by the first time

( ) 39. He will have learned English for eight years by the time he _____ from the university next year.
   A. will graduate   B. will have graduated
   C. graduates   D. is to graduate

( ) 40. The moment the 28th Olympic Games _____ open, the whole world cheered.
   A. declared   B. have been declared
   C. have declared   D. were declared

第十五节　名词性从句

在复合句中起名词作用的从句叫作名词性从句，包括主语从句、宾语从句、表语从句和同位语从句。如：

It is a fact that English is being accepted as an international language.
英语正被接受为一门国际性语言，这是一个事实。（主语从句）
Do you remember how he came?
你记得他是怎么来的吗？（宾语从句）
The trouble is that she has lost his address.
麻烦的是她把他的地址丢了。（表语从句）
I have heard the news that our team had won.
我听到了我们队赢了的消息。（同位语从句）

一、主语从句

1. 概述。

作句子主语的从句叫主语从句。

2. 构成。

主语从句的引导词——连词：that, whether, if；连接代词：what, who, which, whatever, whoever；连接副词：how, when, where, why 等。

3. 用法。

（1）that, whether 引导的主语从句。

That he is still alive is a wonder.

他还活着，真是奇迹。

Whether they will succeed is still a question.

他们是否会成功还是一个问题。

（2）what, who, which, whatever, whichever, whoever, whose 等连接代词引导的主语从句。

What caused the accident is still unknown.

什么引起的这起事故还不得而知。

Whoever wants the book may have it.

任何人想要这本书都可以拿去。

（3）when (ever), where (ever), how (ever), why, how long, how often, how soon, how far, how many/much 等连接副词引导的主语从句。

When we arrive doesn't matter.

我们什么时候到没有关系。

Where the English evening will be held has not yet been announced.

英语晚会将在哪里举行，还没有宣布。

（4）it 作形式主语的句型。

有时为了考虑句子平衡，通常在主语从句处使用形式主语 it，而将真正的主语从句移至句末。

It is known to us that he will come here.

我们都知道他要来这儿。

It remains a secret how they climbed up the mountain.

他们是怎么登上山顶的仍是个秘密。

二、宾语从句

1. 概述。

在复合句中用作宾语的从句叫宾语从句。

2. 构成。

宾语从句的引导词有——连词：that, whether, if；连接代词：who, whose, what, which；连接副词：when，where, how, why 等。

3. 用法。

(1) that 引导宾语从句，that 一般可以省略。

He told me that he would go to the college the next year.

他告诉我他明年上大学。

I heard that he joined the army.

我听说他参军了。

(2) that 引导的宾语从句中的否定转移。

当主句的主语是第一人称，谓语动词是 think, believe, suppose, expect 等动词，其后的宾语从句若含有否定意义，一般要把否定词转移到主句谓语上，从句谓语用肯定式。

I don't think he can do it better than me.

我想他不会干得比我好。

I don't believe you will finish the work today.

我认为你今天无法完成工作。

(3) whether 和 if 引导的宾语从句，两词可以互换，但是在下列情况中只能用 whether，不能用 if。

①在具有选择意义，尤其是直接与 or not 连用时，往往用 whether。

Let me know whether he will come or not.

告诉我他是否要来。

②在介词之后用 whether。

I'm thinking of whether we should go to see the film.

我正在考虑我们是否应该去看电影。

③在不定式前用 whether。

We decided whether to walk there.

我们已决定是否步行去那儿。

④whether 置于句首时，不能换用 if。

Whether this is true or not, I can't say.

这是否是真的我说不上来。

(4) who, whom, whose, which, what 等连接代词引导的宾语从句，连接代词在句中担任主语、宾语、定语或者表语的成分。

Do you know who has won Red Alert game?

你知道是谁赢得了红警游戏吗？

(5) when, where, why, how 等连接副词引导的宾语从句，连接副词在句中担任状语的成分。

He didn't tell me when we should meet again.

他没有告诉我什么时候我们能再见面。

三、表语从句

1. 概述。

在复合句中作表语的从句叫表语从句。

2. 构成。

表语从句一般放在系动词之后，结构是"主语＋系动词＋表语从句"。

表语从句的引导词有——连词：that, whether, as, as if/as though；连接代词：who, whom, whose, what, which；连接副词：when, where, how, why, because 等。

3. 用法。

（1）that 引导表语从句本身没有词义，在句中只起连接作用，不充当句子成分，一般不能省略。

The fact is that more than seventy percent of the earth's surface is covered by water.

事实是地球超过70%的面积是由水覆盖的。

（2）whether 引导表语从句表示"是否"，但不充当句子的成分。whether 与 if 均意为"是否"，但引导表语从句时，只能用 whether，不能用 if。

The question is whether we can finish our work by tomorrow evening.

问题是我们能否在明晚前完成工作。

（3）who, whom, whose, what, which 等代词引导表语从句，在从句中作主语、宾语、表语和定语。

Tom is no longer what he used to be.

汤姆不再是过去的样子了。

（4）when, where, how, why, because 等副词引导表语从句，在从句中作状语。

The question is where we can live.

问题是我们能住在哪儿。

（5）why 和 because 都可以引导表语从句，常用在 It/That is ＋ why/because…句型中，前者强调结果，后者强调原因。

He was ill. That's why he was sent to the hospital.

他病了，所以被送到医院来。

He was sent to hospital. That's because he was ill.

他被送到医院，是因为他病了。

四、同位语语从句

1. 概述。

在复合句中充当同位语的名词性从句称为同位语从句。

2. 构成。

同位语从句一般放在某些名词之后，对前面的名词或代词进行补充说明。

同位语从句的引导词有——连接词 that, whether；连接代词 what, who, whom, whose 和连接副词 how, when, where 等。（注：if, which 不能引导同位语从句。）

3. 用法。

（1）that 引导同位语从句，that 通常不省略。

The idea that you can do this work well without thinking is quite wrong.

你认为不动脑筋就能做好这件工作的想法是完全错误的。

He got the news from Mary that the sports meeting was put off.

他从玛丽那儿得知运动会被推迟的消息。

（2）whether 引导同位语从句。

The question whether we should call in a specialist was answered by the family doctor.

我们是否请专家由家庭医生来定。

（3）what，who，whom，whose 引导同位语从句，在从句中作主语、宾语、表语和定语。

I have no idea what size shoes she wears.

我不知道她穿几号的鞋。

The question who will take his place is still not clear.

谁将取代他的位置现在还不清楚。

（4）when，where，how，why 引导同位语从句，在从句中作状语。

We haven't yet settled the question where we are going to spend our summer vacation.

到哪儿去度暑假，这个问题我们还没有决定。

It's a question how he did it.

问题是他是如何做这件事的。

（5）分隔式同位语从句。

有时同位语从句可以不紧跟在说明的名词后面，而被别的词隔开。

The thought came to him that maybe the enemy had fled the city.

他突然想起可能敌人已经逃出城了。

真题分析

1. I can' remember _____ .
   A. where did I put my keys   B. what I put my keys
   C. where I put my keys   D. what did I put my keys

   分析：我不记得我把钥匙放在什么地方了。考查宾语从句。特殊疑问句作宾语从句应用陈述语序：特殊疑问词＋主语＋谓语＋其他。where 什么地方，故选 C。

2. The school library is _____ we can read many books and magazines.
   A. what   B. where   C. when   D. which

   分析：考查表语从句的连词。学校图书馆是我们能够看书看杂志的地方。What（什么），where（哪里），when（什么时候），which（哪一个）。we can read many books and magazines 修饰主语，是一个表语从句。图书馆是一个地方，连接词用 where，故选 B。

3. It _____ that everyone _____ to laugh.
   A. seems; loves   B. seem; love   C. seems; love   D. seem; loves

   分析：好像每个人都喜欢笑。It seems that…好像，似乎，that 引导的主语从句，it 为形式主语；love to do sth. 喜欢做……根据句意，故选 A 。

4. _____ breaks the school windows will be in for trouble.
   A. Whoever   B. Who   C. Which   D. Whose

   分析：无论谁打破学校的窗户都会有麻烦的。A. Whoever 无论谁，任何人，指人；B. Who 谁，指人；C. Which 哪一个，指物；D. Whose 谁的，后面常跟所修饰的名词，根据句中结构此处缺少主语，指人，whoever 放在句中句子才通顺，who 放在句中句子翻译不通，故选 A。

5. That is _____ we were late last time.
　　A. that　　　　B. when　　　　C. why　　　　D. what

　　分析：这就是上次我们为什么迟到的原因。A. 没有实际意义；B. 当……时候；C. 为什么；D. 什么。为什么迟到，用 why 引导名词性从句，做表语，故选 C。

实战演练

(　　) 1. It's a pity _____ we can't go skating.
　　　　A. what　　　B. that　　　C. where　　　D. /

(　　) 2. _____ surprised me was that he was there.
　　　　A. When　　　B. That　　　C. What　　　D. Which

(　　) 3. It remains a secret _____ they climbed up the mountain.
　　　　A. that　　　B. because　　　C. for　　　D. how

(　　) 4. _____ we do must be in the interest of the people.
　　　　A. What　　　B. That　　　C. Whoever　　　D. Whatever

(　　) 5. It is not clear _____ the crisis（危机）will soon be over.
　　　　A. since　　　B. what　　　C. why　　　D. whether

(　　) 6. It looks _____ it's going to rain.
　　　　A. if　　　B. whether　　　C. as if　　　D. when

(　　) 7. What the doctor is uncertain about is _____ my mother will recover from the serious disease soon.
　　　　A. when　　　B. how　　　C. whether　　　D. why

(　　) 8. The reason I didn't go to Beijing was _____ a new job.
　　　　A. I got　　　　　　　　　B. that I got
　　　　C. because I got　　　　　D. because my getting

(　　) 9. I know nothing about the young man _____ he is from Shanghai.
　　　　A. except that　　B. except for　　C. except　　　D. besides

(　　) 10. _____ you can succeed in the end will depend on _____ you do and _____ you do it.
　　　　A. That; whether; how　　　　B. Whether; what; how
　　　　C. Whether; how; why　　　　D. If; what; why

(　　) 11. They pretended _____ they knew how to do it.
　　　　A. what　　　B. it　　　C. if　　　D. /

(　　) 12. I have no idea _____ or not he has finished the work.
　　　　A. if　　　B. which　　　C. whether　　　D. that

(　　) 13. —I prefer to stay at home and listen to music all day on Sunday.
　　　　—That's _____ I don't agree. You should have a more active life.
　　　　A. what　　　B. how　　　C. when　　　D. where

(　　) 14. The fact has surprised many scientists _____ the earth is becoming warmer and warmer these years.

  A. which B. though C. that D. what

(   ) 15. She is very important to us. We have prepared to do _____ it takes to save her life.

  A. whichever B. however C. whatever D. wherever

(   ) 16. As soon as she comes back, I will tell her when _____ and see her.

  A. you will come   B. do you come

  C. you come   D. will you come

(   ) 17. Someone is knocking at the door, go and see _____ .

  A. who is he B. who he is C. who it is D. who is it

(   ) 18. Obviously _____ we do some exercises every day _____ us good.

  A. that; do B. that; does C. if; do D. what; does

(   ) 19. The reason _____ I have to go is _____ my mother is ill in bed.

  A. why; why B. why; because C. that; because D. why; that

(   ) 20. _____ a computer works is a question that _____ can understand.

  A. What; none   B. How; no one

  C. How; not everyone   D. What; nobody

第十六节 定语从句

一、概述

  定语从句在句中作定语，修饰一个名词或代词，即先行词。定语从句通常出现在先行词后，由关系代词或关系副词引出。常见的关系代词有 that, which, who, whom, whose 等，关系副词有 when, where, why 等。

二、限制性定语从句与非限制性定语从句

  1. 限制性定语从句与非限制性定语从句的区别。

  限制性定语从句对先行词起修饰限制作用；非限制性定语从句对先行词起补充说明作用。非限制性定语从句中，先行词与定语从句往往由逗号隔开。非限制性定语从句相当于并列句、状语从句等。如：

  She has two daughters, who study in the same college.

  (She has only two daughters.)

  她有两个女儿，她们在同一所大学读书。

  She has two daughters who study in the same college.

  (Perhaps she has more than two daughters.)

  她有两个在同一所大学读书的女儿。

  2. 非限制性定语从句中关系代词和关系副词的用法。

  (1) 关系代词和关系副词在任何情况下都不能省略。

That is Bob's mother, who works in a military hospital.

那是鲍勃的妈妈，她在一家军队医院工作。

（2）在非限制性定语从句中 who，whom，which 不能用 that 代替，也不能互相替换。

I saw a movie yesterday, which I think was very interesting.

我昨天看了一部电影，我认为它很有趣。

（3）在"介词＋which/whom 从句"结构中，介词不能放到从句的后面。

This is the house in which she lived 20 years ago.

这是她 20 年前住过的房子。

三、关系代词的用法（表 14）

表 14　关系代词的用法

关系代词从句 格	用于限制性和非限制性 定语从句		只用于限制性 定语从句
	指人	指物	既指人又指物
主格	who	which	that
宾格	whom		
属格	whose/of whom	whose/of which	whose

四、关系代词 that 和 which 的用法

1. 限制性定语从句中，必须用关系代词 that 的情况。

（1）当先行词是 something，somebody，anything，everything，nothing，all，much，little，none，the one 等不定代词时，关系代词只用 that。

Do you have anything that you want to give to your mother?

你有什么想给你妈妈的吗？

I have told you all that I know.

我所知道的都告诉你了。

（2）当先行词前面有 the only，the very，any，few，little，no，all 等词修饰时，关系代词只用 that。

This is the very book that I'm looking for.

这正是我要找的书。

（3）当先行词是形容词最高级或先行词的前面有形容词最高级修饰时，关系代词只用 that。

She is the most beautiful lady that I have ever met.

她是我见过的最漂亮的女士。

（4）当先行词是序数词或有序数词修饰时，关系代词只用 that。

What is the first English novel that you have read?

你读过的第一本英文小说是什么？

(5) 当先行词既有人又有物时,关系代词只用 that。
Do you know the things and persons that they are talking about?
你知道他们正在谈论的人和事吗?
(6) 当先行词在主句中作表语,而关系代词在从句中也作表语时,关系代词只用 that。
Shijiazhuang is no longer the city that it used to be.
石家庄不再是过去的那个城市了。
2. 当先行词指人或指物时,定语从句中的关系词必须用 which 的情况。
(1) 在非限制性定语从句中,只用 which,不能用 that。
My house, which I brought last, has got a lovely garden.
我最后买的那幢房子有一个漂亮的花园。
(2) 当动词短语中的介词提前时,只用 which,不能用 that。
This is the college from which she graduated.
这就是她毕业的那所大学。

五、关系代词 who, whom, that 和 whose 的用法

1. 当先行词指人并在句中作主语时,用 who 或 that。
He is the teacher who/that taught me maths in the university.
他就是大学里教我数学的那位老师。
2. 当先行词指人并在句中作宾语时,用 who, whom 或 that。
That is the little boy who/whom/ that I like best.
那就是我最喜欢的小男孩。
3. 当先行词指人并在定语从句中作定语时,用 whose,不能省略。
This is the car whose window was broken last night.
这就是昨晚车窗被打破的那辆车。

六、关系副词的用法(表 15)

表 15 关系副词的用法

从句	关系副词	用于限制性和非限制性定语从句
时间		when
地点		where
原因		why

Do you remember the day when we first met?
你还记得我们第一次见面的那一天吗?
Can you tell me the office where your father works?
你能告诉我你父亲工作的办公室吗?
This is the reason why I was late for the meeting.

这就是我开会迟到的原因。

七、关系代词 as 引导的定语从句

关系代词 as 既可以引导限制性定语从句，也可以引导非限制性定语从句，as 在句中作主语、宾语或表语。

We have found such materials as are used in the factory.
我们找到了工厂里使用的那种材料。

This film is not such as I expect.
这部电影不像我想象的那样。

He is not the same person as he was.
他已经不是过去的那个他了。

真题分析

1. The girl _____ an English song in the next room is Tom's sister.
   A. who is singing   B. is singing   C. sang   D. was singing
   分析：正在隔壁房间唱英文歌曲的女孩是汤姆的姐姐。这里使用了定语从句，先行词是 the girl，定语从句中缺少主语，用 who 或 that 引导定语从句，故选 A。

2. This is the book _____ tells many English stories.
   A. what   B. which   C. who   D. when
   分析：这是那本讲述很多英语故事的书。此处定语从句修饰先行词 book，故排除 what、who 和 when，此处关系代词 which 在定语从句中作主语。故选 B。

3. Yesterday Li Ming went to the village _____ his family lived ten years ago.
   A. when   B. which   C. where   D. that
   分析：昨天李明去了他家十年前住的村子。定语从句修饰的先行词是 the village，关系词在定语从句中作状语，where 符合题意，故选 C。

4. —Do you know the boy _____ father is from Japan?
   —Yes, his name is Mike.
   A. whom   B. who   C. which   D. whose
   分析：——你认识那个其父亲来自日本的男孩吗？——是的，他的名字叫迈克。考查定语从句。先行词 the boy 是人，不可用指物的 which，可排除 C。who 和 whom 人称代词，空格后有名词 father，所以空格需填物主代词 whose。根据句意结构，可知选 D。

5. The lady _____ spoke to me in the shop is my aunt.
   A. which   B. who   C. where   D. what
   分析：在商店与我说话的那位女士是我的姑姑。A. which 哪一个；B. who 谁；C. where 在哪儿；D. what 什么。The lady 为先行词，指人，引导词用 who 或 that，故选 B。

实战演练

( ) 1. —Did you see any foreigner present at the party?
    —He was the only foreigner _____ I saw at the party.

A. whom　　B. that　　　　　　C. which　　　　　　D. who

( ) 2. After tonight, he would never be the same man _____ he was before.
A. what　　B. who　　　　　　C. as　　　　　　　D. but

( ) 3. The science of medicine, _____ progress has been very rapid lately, is perhaps the most important of all the sciences.
A. to which　　B. in which　　　C. which　　　　　D. with which

( ) 4. By the way, the business friend of mine _____ seems to have changed his mind about coming with you.
A. with who you had lunch　　　B. that you had lunch
C. whom you had lunch　　　　D. you had lunch with

( ) 5. The goals _____ he had fought all his life no longer seemed important to him.
A. after which　　　　　　　　B. with which
C. at which　　　　　　　　　D. for which

( ) 6. Mr. Smith will take a direct route to your house and should arrive about eleven _____ you can talk everything over.
A. when　　B. whom　　　　　C. where　　　　　D. of which

( ) 7. After graduating from New York City College, Professor White continued his studies at Newcastle University, _____.
A. who received his degree in arts　　B. for which he received his degree in arts
C. where he received his degree in arts　D. he received his degree in arts

( ) 8. The events and people _____ in this film are really interesting.
A. that are described　　　　　　B. which are described
C. whom they described　　　　　D. who are described

( ) 9. Mr. Harris, _____ on Sundays, owns two factories.
A. for who I work　　　　　　　B. whom I work
C. that I work　　　　　　　　　D. for whom I work

( ) 10. Books to be renewed should be brought to the desk _____ they are borrowed.
A. in which　　　　　　　　　　B. on which
C. from which　　　　　　　　　D. from where

( ) 11. Sometimes questions _____ meanings seem perfectly obvious to some students are not clearly understood by others.
A. which　　B. their　　　　　C. those　　　　　D. whose

( ) 12. _____ is well known, oceans cover more than 70% of the earth.
A. It　　　B. What　　　　　C. All that　　　　D. As

( ) 13. This is the first university _____ was established in the country.
A. it　　　B. that　　　　　　C. which　　　　　D. As

( ) 14. I sent invitations to 20 people, _____ have replied.
A. of who only 10 of these　　　B. only 10 who
C. of whom only 10　　　　　　D. only 10 of who

(   ) 15. The only way _____ we can help is to give him some money.
　　　　A. which　　　　B. as　　　　C. where　　　　D. that

(   ) 16. Thomas Jefferson's home, _____, sits on a hill overlooking the Washington DC. area.
　　　　A. in which he designed and built　　B. where he designed and built
　　　　C. whose design he built　　　　　　D. which he designed and built

(   ) 17. The machine has a number of functions, _____ are known to us.
　　　　A. some of them　　　　　　　　　B. that some of them
　　　　C. of which some of them　　　　　D. some of which

(   ) 18. Do you know the reason _____ he was absent?
　　　　A. that　　B. who　　C. why　　D. which

(   ) 19. Though time flies, I still clearly remember the days _____ we lived in Beijing.
　　　　A. when　　B. that　　C. where　　D. which

(   ) 20. The Great Wall is one of the most world-famous buildings _____ draw a lot of visitors.
　　　　A. that　　B. which　　C. who　　D. where

第十七节　感叹句

一、感叹句的定义

感叹句是表示喜怒哀乐等强烈情感的句子，有多种表现形式，有时一个单词、短语或一个词组也可成为感叹句。如：Hello！（喂！），The design and the colours！（多美丽的图案和色彩啊！）；有时陈述句、疑问句以及祈使句也可以转化成感叹句，如：What a nice boy！（多好的孩子啊！）How can you be so silly！（你怎么这么傻！）Don't go with us！（别跟我们一起去！）。尽管感叹句的表现形式多种多样，但主要的表现形式只有两种，即 what 和 how 引导的感叹句。what 修饰名词（名词前可加冠词和形容词），how 修饰形容词、副词或动词。

二、感叹句的结构

（一）由感叹词 what 引导的感叹句

1. What + a/an +（形容词）+ 单数可数名词 + 主语 + 谓语！
What a fine day it is！
多好的天气啊！
What an honest girl she is！
她是一个多么诚实的女孩啊！

2. What +（形容词）+ 可数名词复数或不可数名词 + 主语 + 谓语！
What kind women they are！
她们是多么善良的女人啊！

What nice music it is!

多么美妙的音乐啊!

(二) 由 How 引导的感叹句 (how 用来修饰形容词、副词或动词)

1. How + 形容词 (副词) + 主语 + 谓语!

How clever the girl is!

这女孩多聪明啊!

How quickly the boy is writing!

这男孩写得多快啊!

How hard the workers are working!

工人们工作得多么努力啊!

2. How + 主语 + 谓语!

How time flies!

时光飞逝!

注意:

a. how 与 what 引导的感叹句中一般情况下可以相互转换,转换后意义不变。

如:What an interesting story it is! = How interesting the story is!

What a beautiful building it is! = How beautiful the building is!

b. 在口语中,感叹句的主语和谓语常常省略。

如:What a nice present!(省略 it is)

How disappointed!(省略 she is 或其他可作本句主语、谓语的词语)

真题分析

1. —Tu Youyou has won the Nobel Prize(诺贝尔奖)。
   —_____ great she is! We Chinese are so proud of her.
   A. What a   B. What   C. How a   D. How

   分析:—屠呦呦已经赢得了诺贝尔奖。—她是多么伟大的人呀!我们中国人以她为自豪。这里考查的是感叹句,其结构是:how + 形容词 + 主语 + 谓语 + 其他;这里 great 是形容词,应用 how 的结构。故选 D。

2. _____ we had at the party!
   A. How wonderful time   B. What wonderful time
   C. How a wonderful time   D. What a wonderful time

   分析:在晚会上我们度过了多么精彩的一段时光啊。Have a good/wonderful time 是固定短语,符合 "What + a/an + 形容词 + 可数名词单数 + 主语 + 谓语!" 这一结构,故选 D。

3. _____ great fun we had in the park!
   A. What a   B. How a   C. What   D. How

   分析:我们在公园玩得多么快乐呀!英语中的感叹句有两类,一类以 what 开头,强调名词,另一类以 how 开头,强调形容词和副词等。本句强调的是不可数名词 fun,故选 C。

4. _____ bad the weather is!
   A. What   B. How a   C. How   D. What a

分析：多么糟糕的天气啊！what 的感叹句型：what + 形容词 + 不可数名词/可数名词复数形式 +（主语 + 谓语）；what + a/an + 形容词 + 可数名词单数 +（主语 + 谓语）。how 的感叹句型：how + 形容词 + 主语 + 谓语。What bad weather（it is）! = How bad the weather is! 根据题意，故选 C。

5. _____ clever the boy is!
   A. What   B. How   C. What a   D. How a

分析：这孩子多么聪明！结构形式是：How + adj.（adv.）+ 主语 + 谓语。the boy 是主语，故选 B。

实战演练

( ) 1. What _____ is!
   A. the clever monkey it   B. a clever monkey it
   C. the clever monkey   D. a clever monkey

( ) 2. _____ fast the boy is running!
   A. What a   B. How a   C. What   D. How

( ) 3. _____ he is!
   A. What a tall boy   B. How high
   C. What a high boy   D. How taller

( ) 4. What _____ they are!
   A. easily   B. easy job   C. easy jobs   D. an easy job

( ) 5. _____ she sings!
   A. How beautifully   B. What beautiful
   C. What beautifully   D. How beautiful

( ) 6. What _____ they are!
   A. beautiful pictures   B. beautifully pictures
   C. a beautiful picture   D. beautifully pictures

( ) 7. What _____!
   A. exciting news it is   B. exciting news they are
   C. an exciting news it is D. excited news it is

( ) 8. _____ beautiful her sister is!
   A. How a   B. What a   C. How   D. What

( ) 9. How _____ the music sounds!
   A. fine   B. pretty   C. well   D. nice

( ) 10. What _____!
   A. wet weather it is   B. a wet weather it is
   C. a wet whether it is D. wet weather they are

( ) 11. How _____ the girl dances!
   A. good   B. nice   C. well   D. better

( ) 12. How _____!

A. heat the water is   B. hot water is
C. the hot water is   D. hot the water is

( ) 13. How _____ this cow looks!
A. stone   B. strongly   C. strength   D. strong

( ) 14. _____ good time we have!
A. What   B. How a   C. How   D. What a

( ) 15. _____ well the girl is playing the piano!
A. How a   B. How   C. What a   D. What

( ) 16. What a tall boy _____!
A. he is   B. it is   C. is he   D. is

( ) 17. How nice _____!
A. the film is   B. film it is
C. film is   D. a film is

( ) 18. _____ brave the boy is!
A. How a   B. What a   C. What   D. How

( ) 19. _____ Peter is jumping!
A. How highly   B. What highly
C. How high   D. What high

( ) 20. _____ good students they are!
A. What an   B. What a   C. How   D. What

第十八节　倒装句

如果把谓语动词放在主语前面，就叫作倒装。将谓语动词完全移至主语之前，称为完全倒装；如果只把助动词或情态动词放在主语之前，称为部分倒装。

一、构成及用法

（一）完全倒装

完全倒装，即将谓语动词完全移至主语之前。英语中构成完全倒装的情形主要有：

1. 以 here, there, now, then, out, in, up, down, off, away 等方向性副词开头的句子，且句子主语是名词时，句子用完全倒装。

Here comes the bus.

公共汽车来了。

Now comes your turn.

现在该你了。

Then came a new difficulty.

这时又产生了一个新的困难。

注：若主语为代词，则不用倒装。如：

The door opened and in she came.

门开了，她走了进来。

2. 将表语和地点状语（多为介词短语）置于句首加以强调时，其后通常用倒装语序。

Among them was my friend Jim.

他们当中就有我的朋友吉姆。

Around the lake are some tall trees.

湖的四周有些高树。

注：在表语置于句首的倒装结构中，要注意其中的谓语应与其后的主语保持一致，而不是与位于句首的表语保持一致。

（二）部分倒装

部分倒装，即将主语与助动词倒置，其结构与一般疑问句大致相同。英语中构成部分倒装的主要情形有：

1. 含否定意义的词（如 never, hardly, seldom, little, few, not until, not, not only, no sooner, no longer, nowhere, by no means 等）置于句首时，其后用部分倒装。

Never have I read such a book.

我从未读过那样的书。

Little do we know his life.

我们对他的生活了解得很少。

By no means should you tell him about it.

你绝不要告诉他这事。

2. only 加状语（副词/介词短语/从句）放在句首时，其后用部分倒装。

Only in this way can you do it well.

只有这样你才能做好。

Only when he returned home did he realize what had happened.

当他回到家里时，才知道出了什么事。

3. so/neither/nor 表示前面所说的情况也适合于后者时，用"so/neither/nor + 助动词 + 主语"这样的倒装句式。

He can sing English songs and so can I.

他会唱英语歌，我也会。

He didn't see the film, and neither did I.

他没有看这部电影，我也没有看。

She is very beautiful and so was her mother when she was young.

她很美，她妈妈年轻时也很美。

4. 当虚拟条件句含有 were, should, had 时，可省略 if，将 were, should, had 置于句首。

Were I Tom (=If I were Tom), I would refuse.

如果我是汤姆，我就会拒绝。

Had I realized that (=If I had realized that), I would have done something.

我要是明白了这一点，我可能会采取某种行动。

5. so...that 结构中，将 so + adj./adv. 置于句首时，其后要用倒装语序。

So cold was the weather that we had to stay at home.

天气太冷，我们只好待在家里。

So fast does light travel that we can hardly imagine its speed.

光速很快，我们几乎没法想象它的速度。

真题分析

1. Look！Here _____ the bus.

    A. come　　　　　B. comes　　　　　C. go　　　　　D. goes

    分析：看！公交车来了。A. come 动词，来；B. comes 动词第三人称单数形式，来；C. go 动词，走；D. goes 动词第三人称单数形式，走。根据语义可知，本句为倒装句，主语为 the bus，单数含义，谓语动词使用动词第三人称单数形式；come here 来这里，而不是 go here 去这里，故选 B。

2. Jim can swim, _____ .

    A. neither can I　　　　　　　　　B. so I can

    C. so can I　　　　　　　　　　　D. so do I

    分析：Jim 会游泳，我也会。A. neither can I 我也不会；B. so I can 我的确会；C. so can I 我也会；D. so do I 我也会，但动词 do 和上句中 can 不一致。根据上文说 Jim 会游泳，下文应该是说我也会，用倒装句，故选 C。

3. Only yesterday _____ find out that his purse was lost.

    A. he was　　　　　B. was he　　　　　C. did he　　　　　D. he did

    分析：昨天他才发现钱包丢了。only + 修饰成分放在句首，句子用倒装结构。根据 only yesterday 可知句子时态是一般过去时，find out 发现，为行为动词，借助于助动词 did 放在主语 he 前面，谓语动词用原形。故选 C。

4. —I never drink coffee.

    —_____ .

    A. So do I　　　　B. So did I　　　　C. Neither did I　　　　D. Neither do I

    分析：——我从来不喝咖啡。——我也是。根据句意我也从来不喝咖啡，应为否定的倒装句；上文是一般现在时，时态要一致，故选 D。

5. Not a single song _____ at yesterday's party.

    A. she sang　　　　B. sang she　　　　C. did she sing　　　　D. had she sung

    分析：昨晚派对上她一首歌都没唱。否定词放在句首，使用倒装句。本题 not a single song 放在了句首，后面使用部分倒装，原句是 She didn't sing a single song at yesterday's party，因此是 did she sing，故选 C。

实战演练

(　　) 1. Only when you have got enough data _____ come to a sound conclusion.

　　　　A. can you　　　B. you can　　　C. would you　　　D. you would

(　　) 2. _____ that this region was so rich in natural resources.

　　　　A. Little he knew　　　　　　　B. Little did he know

　　　　C. Little he did know　　　　　D. Little he had known

( ) 3. Never again _____ political office after his 1928 defeat for the presidency.
   A. Alfred E. Smith seriously sought
   B. seriously Alfred E. Smith sought
   C. when did Alfred E. Smith seriously seek
   D. did Alfred E. Smith seriously seek

( ) 4. Only in recent years _____ begun to realize that wild dogs often do more good than harm.
   A. people have   B. since people have
   C. have people   D. people who have

( ) 5. —Rita has been to Tokyo twice.
   —_____.
   A. So Lily has.   B. So has Lily.
   C. Lily has so.   D. Lily so has.

( ) 6. Not until I shouted at the top of my voice _____ his head.
   A. that he turned   B. did he turn
   C. he didn't turn   D. he had turned

( ) 7. _____ received law degrees as today.
   A. Never so women have   B. The women aren't ever
   C. Women who have never   D. Never have so many women

( ) 8. Heat does not travel by convection (对流) in solid, because the solid does not move, _____.
   A. so does a liquid   B. so a liquid does
   C. as does a liquid   D. so is a liquid

( ) 9. —They go to school early in the morning.
   —_____
   A. So do Tom.   B. So Tom do.
   C. So does Tom.   D. So Tom does.

( ) 10. —Can you tell me _____?
   —It's Gina, she has changed a lot.
   A. who is she   B. who she is
   C. how she changed   D. whom she is

( ) 11. For a moment nothing happened, then _____ all shouting together.
   A. voices had come   B. came voices
   C. voices would come   D. did voices come

( ) 12. At the foot of the mountain _____.
   A. a village lie   B. lies a village
   C. does a village lie   D. lying a village

( ) 13. In the dark forest _____.
   A. stand many lakes   B. lie many lakes

C. many lakes lie   D. many lakes stand

( ) 14. —Did you see who the driver was?
—No, so quickly _____ that I couldn't get a good look at his face.
A. did the car speed by   B. the car sped by
C. does the car speed by   D. the car speeds by

( ) 15. Mary never does any reading in the evening, _____.
A. so does John   B. John does so
C. John doesn't, too   D. nor does John

( ) 16. Little _____ about her own safety, though she was in great danger herself.
A. did Rose care   B. Rose did care
C. Rose does care   D. does Rose care

( ) 17. I've tried very hard to improve my English. But by no means _____ with my progress.
A. the teacher is not satisfied   B. is the teacher not satisfied
C. the teacher is satisfied   D. is the teacher satisfied

( ) 18. Not until I came home last night _____ to bed.
A. Mum did go   B. did Mum go
C. went Mum   D. Mum went

( ) 19. Only after my friend came _____.
A. did the computer repair   B. he repaired the computer
C. was the computer repaired   D. the computer was

( ) 20. Only then _____ how much damage had been caused.
A. she realized   B. she had realized
C. had she realized   D. did she realize

第十九节　主谓一致

在英语句子里，谓语受主语支配，其动词必须和主语在人称与数上保持一致，这就叫主谓一致。寻其规律，大致可归纳为三个原则，即语法一致、逻辑意义一致和就近一致原则。

一、语法一致原则

语法一致就是谓语动词和主语在单、复数形式上保持一致。

1. 以单数名词或代词、动词不定式短语、动名词短语或从句作主语时，谓语动词一般用单数形式；主语为复数时，谓语动词用复数形式。如：

His father is working on the farm.
他的父亲在农场工作。
To study English well is not easy.
学好英语不容易。

What he said is very important for us all.

他说的话对我们大家都很重要。

The children were in the classroom two hours ago.

两个小时前孩子们还在教室里。

Reading in the sun is bad for your eyes.

在阳光下看书对你的眼睛有害。

注意：由 what 引导的主语从句，后面的谓语动词多数情况下用单数形式，但若表语是复数或 what 从句是一个带有复数意义的并列结构时，主句的谓语动词用复数形式。如：

What I bought were three English books.

我买的是三本英语书。

What I say and do are helpful to you.

我所说的和所做的对你是有帮助的。

2. 由连接词 and 或 both…and 连接起来的合成主语后面，要用复数形式的谓语动词。如：

Lucy and Lily are twins.

露西和莉莉是双胞胎。

She and I are classmates.

她和我是同班同学。

The boy and the girl were surprised when they heard the news.

男孩和女孩听到这个消息时都很惊讶。

Both she and he are Young Pioneers.

她和他都是少先队员。

注意：

（1）若 and 所连接的两个词是指同一个人或物时，它后面的谓语动词就应用单数形式。如：

The writer and artist has come.

那位作家兼艺术家来了。

The singer and songwriter is dead.

这位歌手兼作曲家死了。

（2）由 and 连接的并列单数主语前如果分别有 no，each，every，more than a (an)，many a (an) 修饰时，其谓语动词要用单数形式。如：

Every student and every teacher was in the room.

每个学生和老师都在房间里。

No boy and no girl likes it.

没有男孩和女孩喜欢它。

3. 主语为单数名词或代词，尽管后面跟有 with，together with，except，but，like，as well as，rather than，more than，no less than，besides 等引起的短语，谓语动词仍用单数形式；若主语为复数，谓语用复数形式。如：

Mr. Green, together with his wife and children, has come to China.

格林先生和他的妻子与孩子来到了中国。

Nobody but Jim and Mike was on the playground.

只有吉姆和迈克在操场上。

She, like you and Tom, is very tall.

她像你和汤姆一样，个子很高。

4. either, neither, each, every 或 no + 单数名词和由 some, any, no, every 构成的复合不定代词，都作单数看待。如：

Each of us has a new book.

我们每个人都有一本新书。

Everything around us is matter.

我们周围的一切都是物质。

注意：

a. 在口语中当 either 或 neither 后跟有"of + 复数名词（或代词）"作主语时，其谓语动词也可用复数。如：Neither of the texts is (are) interesting.

b. 若 none of 后面的名词是不可数名词，它的谓语动词就要用单数；若它后面的名词是复数，它的谓语动词用单数或复数都可以。如：

None of the money is mine.

这些钱没有一分钱是我的。

None of us has (have) been to America.

我们中没有一个人去过美国。

5. 在定语从句中，关系代词 that, who, which 等作主语时，其谓语动词的数应与句中先行词的数一致。如：

He is one of my friends who are working hard.

他是我努力工作的朋友之一。

He is the only one of my friends who is working hard.

他是我朋友中唯一努力工作的人。

6. 如果集体名词指的是整个集体，它的谓语动词用单数；如果指集体的成员，其谓语动词就用复数形式。这些词有 family, class, crowd, population 等。如：

Class Four is on the third floor.

四班在三楼。

Class Four are unable to agree upon a monitor.

四班在班长的人选上意见不一。

注意：people, police, cattle 等名词一般都用作复数。如：

How many people were at the meeting?

有多少人到会？

The police are looking for the lost child.

警察正在寻找丢失的孩子。

7. 由"a lot of, lots of, plenty of, the rest of + 名词"构成的短语以及由"分数或百分数 + 名词"构成的短语作主语，其谓语动词的数要根据短语中后面名词的数而定。如：

There are a lot of people in the classroom.

教室里有很多人。

The rest of the lecture is wonderful.
这堂课的其余部分很精彩。
50% of the students in our class are girls.
我们班 50% 的学生是女生。
注意：a number of "许多"，作定语修饰复数名词，谓语用复数；the number of "……的数量"，主语是 number，谓语用单数。

8. 在倒装句中，谓语动词的数应与其后的主语一致。如：
There comes the bus.
公共汽车来了。
On the wall are many pictures.
墙上有许多图画。
Such is the result.
这就是结果。
Such are the facts.
这就是事实。

二、逻辑意义一致原则

逻辑意义一致就是谓语动词的数必须和主语的意义一致（因有时主语形式为单数，但意义为复数；有时形式为复数，但意义为单数）。

1. what, who, which, any, more, all 等代词可以是单数，也可以是复数，主要靠意思来决定。如：
Which is your bag?
哪个是你的包？
Which are your bags?
哪些是你的包？
All is going well.
一切都很顺利。
All have gone to Beijing.
他们都去北京了。

2. 表示"时间、重量、长度、价值"等的名词的复数作主语时，谓语动词通常用单数形式，这是由于作主语的名词在概念上是一个整体，如：
Thirty minutes is enough for the work.
做这项工作 30 分钟足够了。
The $10,000 was lost.
10 000 美元找不到了。

3. 若英语是书名、片名、格言、剧名、报名、国名等的复数形式，其谓语动词通常用单数形式。如：
"*The Arabian Nights*" is an interesting story-book.
《一千零一夜》是一本有趣的故事书。

The United States is a developed country.

美国是一个发达国家

4. 表数量的短语 "one and a half" 后接复数名词作主语时，其谓语动词可用单数形式，也可用复数。如：

One and a half apples is (are) left on the table.

桌子上还剩下一个半苹果。

5. 算式中表示数目（字）的主语通常作单数看待，其谓语动词采用单数形式。如：

Twelve plus eight is twenty.

12 加 8 等于 20。

Fifty-six divided by eight is seven.

56 除以 8 等于 7。

6. 一些以 -ics 结尾的学科名词，如：mathematics，politics，physics 以及 news，works 等，都属于形式上是复数的名词，实际意义为单数名词，它们作主语时，其谓语动词要用单数形式。如：

The paper works was built in 1990.

这家造纸厂建于 1990 年。

I think physics isn't easy to study.

我认为物理不容易学习。

7. trousers, glasses, clothes, shoes 等词作主语时，谓语用复数，但如果这些名词前有 a (the) pair of 等量词修饰时，谓语动词用单数。如：

My glasses are broken.

我的眼镜坏了。

The pair of shoes under the bed is his.

床底下的那双鞋是他的。

8. "定冠词 the + 形容词或分词"，表示某一类人时，动词用复数。

The old are well taken care of.

老人被照顾得很好。

The wounded were all treated.

伤员都得到了救治。

三、就近一致原则

在英语句子中，有时谓语动词的人称和数与最近的主语保持一致。

1. 当两个主语由 either...or, neither...nor, whether...or..., not only...but also 连接时，谓语动词和邻近的主语一致。如：

Either the teacher or the students are our friends.

不是老师就是学生是我们的朋友。

Neither they nor he is wholly right.

他们和他都不是完全正确的。

Is neither he nor they wholly right?

他和他们都不是完全正确的吗?

2. there be 句型中 be 动词单复数取决于其后的主语。如果其后是由 and 连接的两个主语,则应与靠近的那个主语保持一致。如:

There are two chairs and a desk in the room.

房间里有两把椅子和一张桌子。

There is a desk and two chairs in the room.

房间里有一张桌子和两把椅子。

注意:Here 引导的句子用法同上。

真题分析

1. —Where _____ your teacher from?
   — Australia.
   A. am   B. is   C. are   D. be

   分析:——你的老师来自哪里?——澳大利亚。此题考查系动词,因为 your teacher 是第三人称单数,故用 is。根据句意,故选 B。

2. She often _____ her classmates with their homework.
   A. help   B. helps   C. is helping   D. helped

   分析:她经常帮助她的同学做作业。根据 often 判断,经常性的动作用一般现在时,主语 she 是第三人称单数,因此动词要用三单形式,故选 B。

3. Everyone except Tom and Jim _____ going to visit some friends in Shenzhen.
   A. is   B. are   C. am   D. be

   分析:除了汤姆和吉姆之外,每个人都会去拜访在深圳的一些朋友。Except 意为"除了",引起的结构跟在主语后面,不能看作是并列主语,主语如是单数,其谓语动词仍然用单数形式,本句主语是 everyone,不定代词,谓语动词用 be 动词单数 is,故选 A。

4. How time flies! Three years _____ really a short time.
   A. was   B. are   C. is   D. be

   分析:时间过得真快啊!三年真的很短。考查主谓一致。在英语句子里,谓语受主语支配,其动词必须和主语在人称和数上保持一致,这就叫主谓一致。表示"时间、重量、长度、价值、距离"等的名词的复数作主语时,谓语动词通常用单数形式,这是由于作主语的名词在概念上是一个整体,如:Thirty minutes is enough for the work. 对于这项工作 30 分钟就够了。故选 C。

5. Neither Suzy nor I _____ afraid of making a speech in public now.
   A. am   B. are   C. is   D. were

   分析:现在无论是苏西还是我都害怕公开演讲。Neither...nor 既不……也不,当连接并列主语时,要遵循就近原则,故选 A。

实战演练

( ) 1. Either Lily or Mike _____ watching TV at present.
   A. were   B. is   C. was   D. are

(   ) 2. Four days _____ enough for me to finish the work, I need a third day.
　　　　A. isn't　　　B. is　　　　　C. aren't　　　　D. are

(   ) 3. —How many lessons do you usually have a day?
　　　　—Six lessons a day. And each of them _____ 40 minutes.
　　　　A. last　　　B. lasts　　　C. have　　　　D. are

(   ) 4. Neither Li Hua nor I _____ a basketball player.
　　　　A. am　　　B. is　　　　C. be　　　　　D. are

(   ) 5. There _____ many new words in lesson one, and it is very difficult.
　　　　A. is　　　B. aren't　　　C. isn't　　　　D. are

(   ) 6. The number of the students in our school _____ 1,300.
　　　　A. is　　　B. are　　　　C. has　　　　D. have

(   ) 7. Chinese _____ my favorite subject.
　　　　A. be　　　B. is　　　　C. am　　　　D. are

(   ) 8. The boy with the two cats _____ when the earthquake rocked the city.
　　　　A. were sleeping　　　　　　B. is sleeping
　　　　C. was sleeping　　　　　　 D. are aisle

(   ) 9. Every one except Hazel and Winne _____ there when the meeting began.
　　　　A. are　　　B. is　　　　C. were　　　　D. was

(   ) 10. That place is not interesting at all. _____ of us wants to go there.
　　　　A. Neither　　B. Both　　C. All　　　　D. Some

(   ) 11. Nobody but John _____ the secret.
　　　　A. know　　B. knows　　C. have know　　D. is

(   ) 12. —What's on the plate? Some eggs and cakes on it?
　　　　—There _____ some eggs and cakes on it.
　　　　A. is　　　B. are　　　　C. was　　　　D. were

(   ) 13. This pair of glasses _____ mine.
　　　　A. are　　　B. be　　　　C. is　　　　　D. will be

(   ) 14. Both Helen and Lill _____ to the party yesterday.
　　　　A. invited　　　　　　　　　B. was invited
　　　　C. had invited　　　　　　　 D. were invited

(   ) 15. —Three months _____ quite a long time.
　　　　—Yes, I'm afraid that he will miss lots of his lessons.
　　　　A. is　　　B. are　　　　C. was　　　　D. were

(   ) 16. In the city the old _____.
　　　　A. take good care of　　　　B. are taken good care of
　　　　C. is taken good care of　　　D. are been taken good care of

(   ) 17. His family _____ all very kind and friendly. His family _____ a happy one.
　　　　A. are; is　　B. is; is　　　C. are; are　　　D. is; are

(   ) 18. The singer and the dancer _____ been to Beijing.

|　　| A. has | B. have | C. are | D. is |

(　) 19. The children in this class each _____ new school bag.
|　　| A. have | B. has | C. has got | D. are having |

(　) 20. All but one _____ here just now.
|　　| A. is | B. was | C. has been | D. were |

(　) 21. The old _____ well looked after by the government in China.
|　　| A. is | B. are | C. has been | D. was |

(　) 22. The secretary and manager _____ very busy now.
|　　| A. is | B. are | C. was | D. were |

(　) 23. Both the secretary and the manager _____ agreed to attend the meeting.
|　　| A. has | B. have | C. are | D. was |

(　) 24. Mike as well as two of his classmates _____ invited to the party.
|　　| A. was | B. were | C. have been | D. had been |

(　) 25. Either he or I _____ going to the teachers' office after class.
|　　| A. am | B. is | C. are | D. will |

(　) 26. Most of his spare time _____ spent in reading.
|　　| A. are | B. were | C. was | D. have been |

(　) 27. This is one of the best novels that _____ appeared this year.
|　　| A. have been | B. has | C. had been | D. have |

(　) 28. Ten thousand dollars _____ quite a large sum.
|　　| A. are | B. is | C. were | D. have |

(　) 29. About 20 percent of the work _____ done yesterday.
|　　| A. are | B. is | C. were | D. was |

(　) 30. Mr. John, together with his children, _____ arrived.
|　　| A. are | B. has | C. is | D. have |

(　) 31. It _____ I who _____ leaving for London.
|　　| A. is; is | B. am; is | C. is; am | D. am; am |

(　) 32. Not only Tony but also his wife _____ fond of watching television.
|　　| A. are | B. were | C. be | D. is |

(　) 33. When and where to build the new factory _____ yet.
　　A. is not decided　　　　B. are not decided
　　C. has not decided　　　D. have not decided

(　) 34. Although the first part of the book is easy, the rest _____.
　　A. are difficult　　　　　B. has proved difficult
　　C. is supposed difficult　D. have been found difficult

(　) 35. That they were wrong in these matters _____ now clear to us all.
|　　| A. is | B. was | C. are | D. were |

第二章 专项练习

第一节 日常交际用语

1. 问候与道别（Greeting and saying goodbye）。
问候
Hi/Hello！喂！
Good morning/afternoon/evening 早上/下午/晚上好。
How are you? 你好吗？
How are you doing? 你怎么样？
How's everything? 情况如何？
How was your weekend? 你周末过得怎么样？
Long time no see! 好久不见了！
道别
Good bye/Bye-bye/Bye. 再见。
Good night. 晚安/再见（晚上分手时用）。
See you. 回见。
See you later/then/soon/tomorrow. 回见/明天见。
I'm afraid I must be leaving/ must be off/have to go now. 恐怕我得走了。
I'm sorry I have to go now. 很抱歉，我必须走了。
I think it's time for us to leave now. 我想我们该走了。
2. 引荐与介绍（Introducing oneself and others）。
My name is Jim. 我的名字叫吉姆。
I'm a student. 我是一名学生。
I'm from China. 我来自中国。
This is Li Ning. 这位是李宁。
This is Mr. /Mrs. /Miss/Ms. Green.
这位是格林先生/夫人/小姐/女士。
Come and meet Tom.
认识认识汤姆。
May I introduce you to my friends?
请允许我把您介绍给我的朋友们好吗？

3. 感谢与道歉（Expressing thanks and making apologies）。

感谢

Thank you (very much). （非常）感谢。

Thanks a lot. /Many thanks. 多谢。

Thank you for help. 谢谢您的帮助。

It's very kind/nice for you. 您真是太好了。

It's a pleasure. 这是我的荣幸。

I'm very glad you enjoyed it. 我很高兴你喜欢它。

道歉

Sorry. /I'm sorry. 对不起。

I'm sorry for/about that. 我为此感到抱歉/难过。

I'm sorry for losing your book. 很抱歉丢了你的书。

I'm sorry to interrupt you. 很抱歉打扰你了。

I'm sorry (that) I'm late. 对不起，我迟到了。

Sorry, I won't do it again. 对不起我不会再做那样的事了。

I'm sorry to have/I'm sorry that I have kept you waiting for a long time. 抱歉让你久等了。

Excuse me , please. 请原谅。

I beg your pardon. 我请求你的原谅。

4. 预约与邀请（Making appointments and invitations）。

预约

Will you be free tomorrow? 明天你有空吗？

What time is convenient for you? 你什么时候方便？

Do you have time this afternoon? 今天下午你有时间吗？

I'm afraid not. I have no time then. 恐怕不行，我那时没有时间。

Shall we meet at 4：30 at the school gate? 我们4：30在学校门口见面好吗？

I'll look out for you (at) about three. 我3点钟左右等你。

邀请

Let's go for a walk? 让我们散步怎样？

What/How about having a swim? 去游泳怎么样？

Will you come to my birthday party? 你能来参加我们的生日聚会吗？

May I invite you to dinner? 我能邀请你共进晚餐吗？

Shall we have dinner together? 一起去吃饭吧？

Shall we have a drink? 我们喝点东西好吗？

5. 祝愿与祝贺（Expressing wishes and congratulations）。

Congratulations! 祝贺你！

Good luck! 祝你好运！

I wish you good luck/success! 祝你好运/成功！

Wish you all the success! 祝你（们）成功！

Have a nice/good time/day! 玩得高兴！

Have a good journey/trip! 旅行愉快!

Best wishes to you! 向你致以最美好的祝愿!

Happy New Year! 新年快乐!

Happy birthday! 生日快乐!

Merry Christmas! 圣诞快乐!

6. 求助与提供帮助（Asking for and offering help）。

求助

Help me please. 请帮帮我。

Can you help me? 你能帮我一下吗?

Can you give me a hand? 能帮我一下吗?

I need your help. 我需要你的帮助。

I have a favor to ask of you. 我有点事情要求您帮忙。

Can you type this letter for me? 你能帮我把这封信打一下吗?

提供帮助

Can I help you? 我能帮你吗?

May I help you? 我可以帮你吗?

What can I do for you? 我可以为你做点什么吗?

Do you want me to help you? 你想要我帮你吗?

Let me take your bags. 我帮你拿包。

Would you like some tea? 你想来些茶吗?

What would you like to eat? 你想吃些什么?

7. 赞同与反对（Expressing agreement and disagreement）。

赞同

Certainly. /Sure. /Of course. 当然可以。

This is a good idea. 这是个好主意。

I/We agree（with you）. 我/我们同意（你的意见）。

I agree to your plan. 我同意你的计划。

I agree to help you. 我同意帮你。

I agree that this is a good plan. 我赞同这是个好计划。

反对

No way. 没门。

No. I don't think so. 不，我认为不是这样的。

I disagree with you. 我不赞同。

I don't agree with you. 我不同意。

I'm afraid not. 恐怕不是。

I don't think you are right. 我认为你错了。

8. 接受与拒绝（Accepting and rejecting）。

接受

No problem. 没问题。

Great! I'd love that. 太好了，我很愿意。

That sounds great. 听上去不错。

I'd very much like you to accept your invitation. 我非常愿意接受你的邀请。

拒绝

I'm afraid I can't accept you. 恐怕我不能接受你的意见。

I really don't want it. 我真的不需要。

I can't make that happen. 我无法满足你的愿望。

I have other business to take care of. 我有别的事。

It's not convenient for me today. 今天不方便。

9. 劝告与建议（Giving advice and making suggestions）。

劝告

It's no use/good crying. 哭是没有用的。

Why don't you do it yourself? 你为什么不自己做呢？

I advise you to see a doctor. 我劝你去看看医生。

You'd better ask him. 你最好问问他。

You need to have a rest. 你要休息一下。

If I were you, I'd phone him now. 如果我是你，我就给他打电话。

建议

You'd better go out for walk. 你最好出去走走。

Let's go and have a look. 让我们去看看。

Should we go now? 我们现在走好吗？

What/How about a picnic this Sunday? 这个周日去野餐怎样？

Why don't you buy a computer? 你为什么不买这台电脑？

Why not go to a movie? 为什么不去看电影？

10. 投诉与责备（Complaining and blaming）。

Miss, the air conditioner in my room doesn't work. 小姐，我这屋里的空调坏了。

Who's supposed to take care of this? 这事由谁来管？

I'm afraid I have to return this sweater. 恐怕我得把这件毛衣退掉。

What do you mean by doing so? 你这么做是什么意思？

He's to blame. 他应该受到责备。

He shouldn't have done it. 他本不应该做这事。

Why didn't you tell me the truth? 你为什么不告诉我实情？

How could you cheat your teacher? 你怎么能欺骗你的老师？

Why don't you do something about it? 你为什么不对此做点什么？

11. 表扬与鼓励（Praising and encouraging）。

表扬

Very good! 非常好！

Well done! 干得好！

Excellent! 太好了！

You speak English very well. 你的英语说得非常好。

Your dress is beautiful. 你的裙子很漂亮.

鼓励

Come on！加油！

Keep trying！继续努力！

You can do it！你能行的！

You are best！你是最棒的！

12. 指令与要求（Giving instructions and making requests）。

Don't rush/hurry. 别急。

Don't crowd. 别挤。

Please stand in line. 请排队。

No noise, please. 请勿喧哗。

No smoking, please. 请勿吸烟。

Make sure of the time and place. 把时间和地点弄清楚。

Can/Will/Could/Would you do it for me? 你能帮我做这件事情吗？

Would you spare me some ink please? 你能给我点墨水吗？

Do you mind if I get a lift in your car, please? 我搭你的车介意吗？

Please give/pass me the pen. 请给/递给我那支笔。

13. 禁止与警告（Prohibiting and warning）。

禁止

You can't/mustn't do that. 你不可以那样做。

You'd better not do it. 你最好别做这件事。

Don't smoke. 禁止吸烟。

Don't be late. 别迟到。

警告

Wet floor！小心地滑！

Look out！当心！留神！

Be careful！小心！

If you don't go right now, you'll be late. 如果你不马上走，你就会迟到。

If you dare do it again, I'll beat you. 如果你敢再做，我就要打你。

I warn you if you do it again, we'll punish you. 我警告你，你再这样做，我们就处分你。

14. 询问与提供信息（Seeking and offering information）。

询问

Excuse me, can you tell me where the railway station is? 劳驾，请问火车站在哪儿?

Excuse me, would you show me the way to the supermarket? 劳驾，请问去超市的路怎么走?

Excuse me, could you give me some directions? 劳驾，请你给我指指路好吗?

Excuse me, could you mind telling me the way to the post office?

劳驾，请告诉我邮局怎么走?

提供信息

It's over there. 就在那边。
It's just around the corner. 就在拐角处。
It's opposite the post office. 在邮局对面。
It's next to the hospital. 就在医院隔壁。
Go down the road and you'll come to a bus stop. 沿着这条路走，你会走到一个公交车站。
Go down this street and turn to the left at the first crossing. 沿着这条街走，在第一个十字路口向左拐。

15. 情感表达（Expressing feelings and emotions）。
That's fine. 很好。
Well done! 干得好！
I'm so happy. 我真高兴。
How nice/wonderful! 好极了！/妙极了！
I'm glad to hear that. 听到这个我很高兴。
Really? 真的？
Oh dear! /Dear me! 哎呀！
I'm so sorry! 我很难过。
I'm surprised. 我感到很吃惊。
It's disappointing! 真令人失望！
What bad luck! 真倒霉！
What's wrong? 怎么了？
Anything wrong? 有什么不对的？

16. 讨价还价（Bargaining）。
Give me a discount! 给我打个折吧！
How much do you want for this? 这件东西你想多少钱买？
Can you give me this for cheaper? 能便宜一点给我吗？
Can you cut down the price for me? 你能给我优惠点吗？
Your prices are too high for us to accept. 你的价格太高，我们不能接受。
Our prices are the most reasonable. 我们的价格是合理的。
This is the lowest possible price. 这是最低价了。

真题分析

1. —Thank you for your help.
   —_____.

   A. That's all right　　　　　　　　B. No, thanks
   C. That's right　　　　　　　　　　D. Of course

   分析：对别人的感谢，一般用"That's all right""不客气"来回答。故选A。

2. —Will you please take a message for the headteacher?
   —_____.

   A. It doesn't matter　　　　　　　　B. Sure, I'll be glad to

C. Yes. I'll take　　　　　　　　　　　D. I can help you

分析：问句的意思是：你能不能给校长捎个口信儿？答句的意思是：当然，我很乐意。故选B。

3. —I'm going to Hainan on vacation next week.
   —_____.
   A. Have a good time　　　　　　　　B. Not at all
   C. Thank you　　　　　　　　　　　D. I have no idea

分析：have a good time 是指"玩得开心，玩得愉快"。故选A。

实战演练

(　　) 1. —How's it going?
    —_____
    A. It's great.　　　　　　　　　　　B. Yes, I'd love to.
    C. I don't think so.　　　　　　　　D. It's a pleasure.

(　　) 2. —Nice to meet you.
    —_____
    A. Fine, thank you.　　　　　　　　B. How do you do?
    C. Nice to meet you, too.　　　　　D. The same to you.

(　　) 3. —My name is Dongdong.
    —What's your name?
    —_____
    A. I'm Li Ming.　　　　　　　　　　B. I'm fine.
    C. Today is sunny.　　　　　　　　D. I like milk.

(　　) 4. —Jim. This in Miss Sophie Dupont.
    —_____
    A. It's great.　　　　　　　　　　　B. I'm fine.
    C. Nice to meet you.　　　　　　　D. Thanks a lot.

(　　) 5. —I'm sorry to trouble you, Miss White.
    —_____
    A. Fine, thank you.　　　　　　　　B. All right.
    C. It doesn't matter.　　　　　　　D. It's very kind of you.

(　　) 6. —We plan to go out for a picnic next weekend. Would you like to come along?
    —_____. It's my favorite.
    A. Enjoy yourself　　　　　　　　　B. It doesn't matter
    C. You're welcome　　　　　　　　D. That would be very nice

(　　) 7. —Would you like to play basketball with us this afternoon?
    —_____. I have to study for tomorrow's test.
    A. I'd love to　　　　　　　　　　　B. I'm afraid not
    C. Sounds good　　　　　　　　　　D. No problem

(　　) 8. —Mike, our team will play against the Rockets this weekend. I'm sure we will win.
—_____!

　　A. Congratulations　　　　　　B. Cheers
　　C. Best wishes　　　　　　　　D. Good luck

(　　) 9. —Merry Christmas!
—_____.

　　A. I'm very happy　　　　　　　B. It's very kind of you
　　C. Thanks. The same to you　　　D. My pleasure

(　　) 10. —Can you help me repair the bike?
—_____. Come and get it in half an hour.

　　A. Of course　　　　　　　　　B. Not at all
　　C. That's all right　　　　　　　D. You're welcome

(　　) 11. —Could I use your bike for today, Sam?
—_____. I'm not using it.

　　A. Sure, go ahead　　　　　　　B. I have no idea
　　C. No, you can't　　　　　　　　D. Never mind

(　　) 12. —Maths is as interesting as English, I think.
—_____. English is more interesting than maths.

　　A. I think so　　　　　　　　　B. I don't think so
　　C. I hope so　　　　　　　　　D. I don't hope so

(　　) 13. —Dirty water shouldn't be poured into rivers.
—_____. It will cause pollution.

　　A. Don't say like this　　　　　B. Never mind
　　C. I agree with you　　　　　　D. The same to you.

(　　) 14. —Would you take this along to the office for me?
—_____.

　　A. With pleasure　　　　　　　B. That's right
　　C. Never mind　　　　　　　　D. Don't mention it

(　　) 15. —Could you do me a favour and take these books to my office?
—Yes, _____.

　　A. for pleasure　　　　　　　　B. I could
　　C. my pleasure　　　　　　　　D. with pleasure

(　　) 16. —How about going to the Disneyland together?
—_____.

　　A. Enjoy yourself!　　　　　　　B. Good luck!
　　C. What's up?　　　　　　　　D. Sounds like a good idea!

(　　) 17. —You'd better not eat too much salt. It's bad for your health.
—_____.

　　A. Not at all　　　　　　　　　B. You're welcome

C. It doesn't matter   D. Thanks for your advice

(　　) 18. —You haven't paid for it yet.

　　　　—_____.

　　　　A. Oh, I'm really very sorry   B. No trouble at all

　　　　C. That's nothing   D. Never mind

(　　) 19. —What a beautiful picture you've drawn!

　　　　—_____.

　　　　A. Not at all   B. Thank you

　　　　C. You are great   D. I'm proud of you

(　　) 20. —I'm thinking of the test tomorrow. I'm afraid I can't pass this time.

　　　　—_____! I'm sure you'll make it.

　　　　A. Go ahead   B. Good luck

　　　　C. No problem   D. Cheer up

(　　) 21. —Don't take pictures here, please.

　　　　—_____.

　　　　A. No way   B. Sorry, I won't

　　　　C. Here you are   D. It's a pleasure

(　　) 22. —Tory, don't draw on the wall. It isn't a good behavior.

　　　　—_____.

　　　　A. Never mind   B. Yes, I'd love to

　　　　C. Of course not   D. Sorry, I won't

(　　) 23. —Look, Jim. Please don't smoke here. It's a no-smoking area.

　　　　—_____.

　　　　A. Never mind   B. Yes. I'd love to

　　　　C. Of course not   D. Sorry, but I didn't see it just now

(　　) 24. —Excuse me. Could you please tell me where I can get the dictionary?

　　　　—_____. There's a bookstore on Yimeng Road.

　　　　A. Sorry   B. Sure   C. Good idea   D. Thank you

(　　) 25. —What's your father?

　　　　—_____.

　　　　A. He's working in Fukang   B. He is always kind to others

　　　　C. He is really a good man   D. He's an engineer

(　　) 26. —I had a really good weekend at my uncle's.

　　　　—_____.

　　　　A. Oh, that's very nice of you   B. Congratulations

　　　　C. It's a pleasure   D. Oh, I'm glad to hear that

(　　) 27. —Betty, you don't look well. What's wrong?

　　　　—I have a fever.

　　　　—_____. You'd better go to see a doctor.

  A. I'm sorry to hear that   B. Oh, mine
  C. It's all right   D. You look bad

( ) 28. —I like this television very much. How much does it cost?
  —It costs five hundred pounds.
  —_____. We can't afford all that money.
  A. That's too cheap for us   B. That's too expensive for us
  C. Is it of good quality   D. Oh, good

( ) 29. —Write to me when you get home.
  —_____.
  A. I must   B. I should   C. I will   D. I can

( ) 30. —Is that Mike speaking?
  —Yes. _____?
  A. Who's this   B. Who's that
  C. Who are you   D. Who's Mike

第二节　完形填空

  完形填空（Cloze Test）是外语学习中的一种综合练习或测试。这种题目提供一篇短文，把文中的若干词语删去，留出空白，要求学生根据全文的意思，把正确的词语填入空白处。要做好完形填空，学生不仅要具备一定的词汇和语法知识，还必须具备一定的阅读理解和综合分析能力，这种题目既考查学生的语言知识水平，又检验学生的分析判断能力和综合运用语言知识的实践能力。

  解题步骤和方法：

  1. 通读全文，领会大意。

  完形填空的特点是提供了完整的文章，让学生在一定的语境中运用所学的外语知识来填空，要求学生在领会文章大意的基础上解题。因此，学生首先要把全文通读一遍，基本了解大意，如果对文章的主要意思还不清楚，宁可再看一遍，再着手填空，切忌看一句填一句。

  每篇短文总有一定的主题思想，段落之间必然能承上启下、前呼后应，句与句之间也一定紧密相连，形成一个有机的整体，先通读全文，掌握文章的逻辑思维，顺着思路去解题，就不难选出正确的答案。

  做好完形填空练习的关键在于抓住文章的主题思想和大意。根据上下文的意思，才能选出正确的答案。如果平时经常阅读英语短文，注意培养自己快速阅读的能力，就能很快捕捉到文章的大意，完成这种练习就不会感到很困难。

  2. 逐句阅读，选出答案。

  在通读一两遍短文、了解大意的基础上，再逐句阅读，选出答案。在选择答案时，可以采用排除法，首先排除在语法上或内容上明显不合乎要求的答案，再细致地鉴别语法正确而词意有别的选项，以确定合适的答案。

  要特别注意文章的第一个句子，"首句"一般都是不带空白的完整的句子，借助这个

"首句",可以大致了解文章的题材内容和文体特点,还可以确定全文所用的动词时态的范围,例如确定是过去时、现在时还是将来时。

3. 复读全文,检查答案。

全部空白填完后,把短文重读一遍,目的是检查答案能否使全文通顺流畅以及用词是否恰当。要从文意和语法知识两个方面进行检查,对自己易犯的错误要特别细心察看,加以避免。例如:名词用单数还是复数,前面用不用冠词,代词的性、数、格,谓语动词的人称和数是否与主语一致,时态、语气、语意是否合适,与名词或动词连用的介词是否正确等。

真题分析

(一)

Mr. Wang teaches English in a middle school. He likes his work very much. He wanted __1__ a teacher even when he was a young boy.

There are six classes in a school day at Mr. Wang's middle school. Mr. Wang teachers five of these six classes. __2__ his "free" hour from 2 to 3 in the afternoon, Mr. Wang __3__ meet with parents, check students' homework and __4__ many other things. So Mr. Wang works hard from the moment he gets to school early in the morning until he leaves for home late in the afternoon, and his "free" hour is not free at all.

In his English lesson, Mr. Wang sometimes teaches poems (诗). He likes poems very much, and he likes Li Bai's poems __5__ of all.

In his fifth class today, Mr. Wang taught a poem. He wrote the poem on the blackboard and read it. As soon as he finished __6__ the poem, the students began to ask questions. He answered all the questions. Then he asked his students to talk about the poem. __7__ one wanted to stop when the bell rang.

__8__ home, Mr. Wang thought about the fifth class. He was happy about what he did as a teacher. Every one of his students __9__ the poem. When they started to talk, they forgot about the time. He did not have to make them __10__. He only had to answer their questions and help them understand the poem.

1. A. was   B. being   C. to be   D. be
2. A. In   B. At   C. To   D. On
3. A. has to   B. has   C. able to   D. will
4. A. take care for   B. care of   C. take care of   D. be careful of
5. A. better   B. good   C. well   D. best
6. A. reading   B. to read   C. read   D. doing
7. A. Not   B. No   C. Have no   D. Any
8. A. By the way B. To his way   C. On his way   D. In the way
9. A. liked   B. asked   C. had   D. wanted
10. A. learning   B. to learn   C. learn   D. leant

分析:Mr. Wang 是一位英语老师,他热心于教育,忙于教学,工作负责,课堂上善于启发学生回答问题、讨论问题。即使在回家的途中，仍沉浸在课堂活跃气氛的回忆中。

1. C。语法结构 want 后面跟不定式。
2. B。时间点后面跟介词 at。
3. A。has to 意思是"不得不，必须"。这里引出所要做的事。
4. C。固定短语。
5. D。此句后面有 of all 这一比较范围，故用最高级。
6. A。finish 后面跟动名词。
7. B。课堂上学生们积极发言，没有人想停下来。
8. C。on one's way home 意思是"在回家的路上"。
9. A。学生受老师的影响也开始爱诗歌了。
10. C。语法结构：make sb. do sth.。

(二)

Have you ever seen the advertisement: Learn a foreign language in six weeks, ___1___ give your money back? Of course, it ___2___ happens quite like that. The only language ___3___ to learn is the mother language. And think ___4___ practice is needed for that. Before the Second World War people usually learned a foreign language ___5___ the literature（文学）of the country. Now most people want to ___6___ a foreign language. Every year millions of people start learning ___7___.

How do they do it? Some people try at home ___8___ books and tapes, others go to evening classes or watch TV programs. ___9___ they use the language only 2 or 3 times a week, learning it will ___10___ a long time, like language learning at school. A few people try to learn a language fast by studying for 6 or ___11___ hours a day. It's much easier to learn the language in the country where it ___12___. But most people are ___13___ to do this, and many people don't have to do so. Machines and good books will be very ___14___, but they can not do the students' work. ___15___ the language is learned quickly or slowly, it is hard work.

1. A. so	B. or	C. and	D. but
2. A. can't	B. impossible	C. never	D. often
3. A. easily	B. difficult	C. able	D. easy
4. A. how much	B. how long	C. how fast	D. how many
5. A. studied	B. to study	C. studying	D. study
6. A. talk	B. tell	C. speak	D. say
7. A. them	B. this	C. that	D. it
8. A. without	B. with	C. in	D. by
9. A. If	B. When	C. Since	D. Until
10. A. spend	B. use	C. take	D. cost
11. A. some	B. more	C. other	D. less
12. A. speaks	B. is speaking	C. spoke	D. is spoken
13. A. able	B. possible	C. unable	D. not possible
14. A. careful	B. forgetful	C. wonderful	D. helpful
15. A. Either	B. Whether	C. What	D. How

分析：本文主要想告诉读者，学英语是一个长期而艰苦的劳动，没有任何捷径可走。无论你用什么方法学习——用书、机器或在学校，不多实践就无法达到预期的目的。

1. B。这里的 or 是"否则"的意思。
2. C。根据作者的观点，这种事绝对不可能发生。impossible 是一个形容词，不符语法，can't 后不可能跟 happens，often 意思与作者的意图相反。
3. D。唯一容易学的语言是母语。这里需要一个形容词充当后置定语。
4. A。用来修饰不可数名词，只有用 how much，全句意为"母语好学，还需要那么多的练习。何况外语呢?"
5. B。动词不定式充当目的状语。意为"学习外语来研究文学"。
6. C。说某种语言用 speak，speak English，speak Chinese。
7. D。用 it 代指上文所说的 a foreign language。
8. B。这里的 with 是"用"的意思。
9. A。作者在这里提出一种假设。如果他们一星期只有一两次使用外语。
10. C。固定短语，意为"做某事花费某人多长时间"。
11. B。后面省略了 than 6 hours。意为 6 个小时或更多的时间。
12. D。it 代指上文所指的 foreign language，故用被动语态。
13. C。许多人不可能做到这一点。这里不可以用 not possible，因为它的主语不可以为人。
14. D。机器和书对于学习英语来说是很有帮助的。
15. B。whether…or…固定短语。

（三）

Long ago there was a poor farmer called Fred. Fred and his wife, Doris lived __1__ together in their small old house. One winter night, the Luck Fairy（仙女）visited them.

"Fred, you're a __2__ farmer. I'd like to give you a wish," said the Luck Fairy.

"A wish?" Said Fred.

Fred and Doris smiled at each other. Then Fred said, "Thank you, Luck Fairy. We're very __3__ and happy."

"__4__ we're old, we still work in the field every day," said Doris.

"You work very hard but you __5__ very little money. Would you like some gold coins?" asked the Luck Fairy.

"Oh no, my dear Luck Fairy. We're poor. But we have __6__ food to eat." replied Fred.

"You can use the gold coin to buy some clothes. The winter here is very cold," said Luck Fairy.

"Though we haven't got __7__ clothes, we've got enough," said Doris.

"Well, what about a nice new house?" asked Luck Fairy.

"Thank you, but I __8__ my small old house very much. I've lived here since I was born. I don't __9__ a new house," said Fred.

"You're quite different from other people. I like you very much," said the Luck Fairy. "I wish you happiness and Luck forever." Then the Luck Fairy __10__ and never came back.

1. A. sadly　　　B. happily　　　C. worried　　　D. anxiously
2. A. bad　　　　B. lazy　　　　C. good　　　　D. unhelpful

3. A. healthy	B. careful	C. difficult	D. important
4. A. If	B. But	C. Because	D. Though
5. A. cost	B. lose	C. make	D. borrow
6. A. no	B. little	C. enough	D. expensive
7. A. old	B. many	C. bad	D. clean
8. A. hate	B. love	C. need	D. dislike
9. A. need	B. see	C. buy	D. build
10. A. smiled	B. nodded	C. laughed	D. disappeared

分析：这则故事告诉我们，人不必贪心，要懂得知足常乐。

1. B。根据下文我们知道，这对夫妇生活得很愉快。
2. C。正因为 Fred 是一个好农夫，仙女才要奖励他。
3. A。比较这四个词的意思不难发现与 happy 并列的是 healthy。
4. D。根据 still 可知选 though。虽然他们年纪大了，但仍然能够在田里干活。
5. C。make money 意思是"赚钱"。
6. C。根据文意，他们对一切都感到知足，包括食物他们也觉得足够吃了。
7. B。他们没有许多衣服，但对他们来说却已经够穿了。
8. B。love，喜欢，喜爱。符合题意。
9. A。根据上文，他们喜欢自己的小屋，所以不需要新的。
10. D。根据 never come back 可知仙女消失了。

实战演练

（一）

We know that trees are useful in our every day life. They ___1___ us many things, such as wood, oxygen, rubber, medicines and many other things. They can ___2___ tell us a lot about our climate (气候). The following are the reasons (理由).

If you ___3___ a tree, you can see that it has many rings (年轮). Most trees grow one new ring ___4___ year. Because of this reason, we know ___5___ a tree is. A tree over a hundred years old means that it has more than a hundred ___6___. When the climate is dry or very cold, the trees do not grow very much and their rings are usually ___7___. When it is wet and warm, the rings are much thicker. If the rings are suddenly very thin or suddenly very thick, this means that the ___8___ changed suddenly. If we look at the rings on this tree, we can learn about the ___9___ for a hundred years. We can see ___10___ our climate is changing today.

1. A. tell	B. ask	C. give	D. get
2. A. not	B. too	C. to	D. also
3. A. cut across	B. climb up	C. walk past	D. look at
4. A. every	B. many	C. the first	D. from
5. A. how big	B. how long	C. how old	D. how much
6. A. trees	B. leaves	C. people	D. rings
7. A. big	B. thick	C. small	D. thin

8. A. climate B. trees C. rings D. animal
9. A. people B. things C. climate D. life
10. A. how B. why C. when D. while

(二)

Mark lived in a village far away. One day he became very ill and everyone thought he would __1__ soon. They sent for a doctor. Two days __2__ the doctor came and looked over the sick man. __3__ asked for a pen and some paper to write down the name of the medicine. But there was no pen __4__ paper in the village, because no one could write.

The doctor __5__ up a piece of burnt wood from the fire and wrote the name of the medicine on the __6__ of the house. "Get this medicine for him." he said, "and he will soon get __7__." Mark's family and friends did not know __8__ to do. They could not read the strange words. Then a young man __9__ an idea. He took off the door of the house, put it on his carriage (马车) and drove to the nearest __10__. He bought the medicine there, and Mark was soon well again.

1. A. wake B. cry C. moved D. die
2. A. late B. later C. ago D. before
3. A. The sick man B. Mark C. The doctor D. The farmer
4. A. and B. or C. then D. also
5. A. picked B. held C. made D. looked
6. A. wall B. window C. ground D. door
7. A. well B. worse C. bad D. good
8. A. when B. what C. where D. which
9. A. thought B. hit C. caught D. had
10. A. shop B. farm C. hospital D. village

(三)

Mary has some friends. __1__ Betty, Peter, Alice __2__ Mike. Mary is the oldest __3__. Betty is thirteen years __4__. She is younger than Mary and older than Peter. Alice is nine and Mike is seven.

Betty and Peter are __5__ runners. But Peter runs faster. Mary and Betty like to __6__. Mary plays better than Betty. Alice sings __7__ of them. Mary and Betty study in a middle school. Alice and Mike study in a primary school. They __8__ work hard at school. But Betty works __9__. Her handwriting is good, __10__.

1. A. They are B. It is C. There are D. We are
2. A. But B. Or C. them D. and
3. A. in the five B. of five C. of the five D. for the five
4. A. older B. old C. oldest D. very old
5. A. best B. better C. well D. good
6. A. play basketball B. play a basketball
   C. play the basketball D. play basketballs
7. A. good B. better C. best D. well

8. A. six	B. all	C. four	D. both
9. A. hard	B. harder	C. very hard	D. hardest
10. A. too	B. two	C. at	D. also

(四)

Someone says, "Time is money", but I think time is __1__ important than money. Why? Because when money is spent, we can get it back. However, when time is __2__, it'll never __3__. That is __4__ we must not waste time. It goes without saying that the __5__ is usually limited. Ever a second is very important. We should make full use of our time to __6__ useful.

But it is a pity that there are a lot of people who do not know the importance of the time. They spent their limited time smoking, drinking and __7__. They do not know that wasting time means wasting part of their own __8__.

In a word, we should save time. We shouldn't __9__ today's work for tomorrow. Remember we have no time to __10__.

1. A. much	B. less	C. mush less	D. even more
2. A. cost	B. bought	C. gone	D. finished
3. A. return	B. carry	C. take	D. bring
4. A. what	B. that	C. because	D. why
5. A. money	B. time	C. day	D. food
6. A. nothing	B. something	C. anything	D. everything
7. A. reading	B. writing	C. playing	D. working
8. A. time	B. food	C. money	D. life
9. A. stop	B. leave	C. let	D. give
10. A. lose	B. save	C. spend	D. take

(五)

Many people think the more time is spent, the more work will be done. So students have to spend the whole __1__ doing school work except the three meals. It is __2__ to see students struggling (挣扎) in a sea of school work both at school and at home.

Modern students usually have many __3__. They love music and sports. They love reading and watching TV. A two-day weekend can get them __4__ from too much school work, and they can do what they like. But still teachers do not think about it. __5__ they have too much school work, they have no time to enjoy themselves. Students are really tired of their weekend homework. So they usually don't do their weekend homework __6__ Sunday night. And there is not enough time but much work, students have to finish it __7__. The weekend homework makes teachers angry.

Things always get __8__ without right ideas. Too much school work makes students lose interest in learning. It's also bad for their health.

A horse runs faster after __9__. But for students only rest is not enough. So such a condition (状况) should be __10__ to give students both pleasure and knowledge.

| 1. A. day | B. morning | C. after | D. week |
| 2. A. never | B. common | C. glad | D. hardly |

3. A. books	B. interests	C. sports	D. friends
4. A. busy	B. pleased	C. away	D. tired
5. A. For	B. With	C. Though	D. Because
6. A. until	B. when	C. at	D. on
7. A. good	B. poor	C. carelessly	D. happy
8. A. better	B. afraid	C. worse	D. wonderful
9. A. minute	B. moment	C. meal	D. rest
10. A. kept	B. changed	C. same	D. different

(六)

A man was sitting in the doctor's office. He was telling the doctor about his __1__. "I like football, doctor." he said. "Please help me. My life has __2__ been a good one since I became __3__ in football and it is getting worse and worse. I can't even __4__ well at night. When I close my __5__, I'm out there in the football field __6__ after a flying ball. When I wake up, I'm more __7__ than I was when I went to bed. What am I going to do?" The doctor sat back and said, "First of all, you __8__ to do your best not to dream about football. Before you are falling asleep, try to __9__ about something else. Try to think that you are at a party and someone is going to give you several million dollars." "Are you crazy?" the man shouted. "I'll __10__ the ball!"

1. A. problem	B. family	C. sport	D. journey
2. A. always	B. already	C. never	D. often
3. A. interested	B. careful	C. deep	D. strong
4. A. work	B. play	C. do	D. sleep
5. A. doors	B. window	C. books	D. eyes
6. A. looking	B. playing	C. running	D. waiting
7. A. worried	B. tired	C. surprised	D. pleased
8. A. want	B. hope	C. have	D. decide
9. A. hear	B. write	C. talk	D. think
10. A. miss	B. play	C. catch	D. pass

(七)

Have you ever asked yourself why children go to school? You may __1__ they go to learn languages, P. E., history, science and all other __2__. But why do they learn these things?

We send our children to school to prepare them for the time __3__ they will grow up and will begin to work for __4__. Nearly everything they study at school has some practical use in their life. But is that the __5__ reason why they go to school?

There is more in education than just __6__ facts. We go to school above all to learn how to learn, so that then we have left school we can __7__ to learn. A man who really knows how to learn will always be successful, because whenever he has to do something new which he has never had to do __8__ he will rapidly teach himself how to do it __9__ the best way. The uneducated person, on the other hand, is __10__ unable to do something new, or does it badly. The purpose of school, therefore, is not to teach languages, math, geography, etc, but to teach pupils the way to learn.

1. A. speak	B. tell	C. say	D. talk
2. A. matters	B. subjects	C. math	D. physics
3. A. while	B. when	C. which	D. where
4. A. oneself	B. they	C. them	D. themselves
5. A. only	B. nearly	C. lonely	D. alone
6. A. study	B. studied	C. learning	D. learn
7. A. make	B. keep	C. keep on	D. go on
8. A. later	B. ago	C. then	D. /
9. A. from	B. in	C. with	D. on
10. A. either	B. neither	C. other	D. nor

(八)

Grandma Li lived alone in an old building. She was old and didn't like noise at all. The young man and woman __1__ always made much noise every night, so she couldn't __2__. When the young man and woman moved out of the building, Grandma Li was very __3__. Another young man moved in and Grandma Li thought, "Well, he __4__."

But at three o'clock the next morning, when Grandma Li __5__, some noise __6__. She __7__ carefully. It was a dog. She thought, "There wasn't any dog here before. It __8__ be the young man's." She __9__ him and telephoned the young man at once. Before the young man could say something, she stopped the call.

Nothing more happened __10__ four o'clock. Then Grandma Li's telephone rang. When she answered the phone, she heard, "I'm the man upstairs. I'm sorry to trouble you, but I want to tell you I don't have a dog at all!"

1. A. upstairs	B. up	C. above	D. higher
2. A. get to sleep	B. sleeps	C. slept	D. falls asleep
3. A. sad	B. pleased	C. surprised	D. worried
4. A. looked quiet	B. looks quiet	C. looked quite	D. looks quite
5. A. was sleeping		B. was falling asleep	
C. slept		D. was getting to sleep	
6. A. woke her up	B. waked she up	C. woke up her	D. waked up she
7. A. heard	B. listened	C. was hearing	D. listened to
8. A. can	B. may	C. must	D. could
9. A. angry with	B. angrier with	C. is angry with	D. was angry with
10. A. when	B. after	C. at	D. until

(九)

When you wave to a friend, you are using sign language. When you smile to someone, you mean to be __1__. When you put one finger in front of your __2__, you mean "Be quiet."

Yet, people in different countries may use different sign languages.

Once an Englishman was in Italy. He could speak __3__ Italian. One day while he was walking in the street, he felt __4__ and went into a restaurant. When the waiter came, the Englishman

5   his mouth, put his fingers into it and took them out again and moved his lips. In this way, he   6   to say, "Bring me something to eat." But the waiter brought him a lot of things to   7   . First tea, then coffee, then milk, but no food. The Englishman was   8   that he was not able to tell the waiter he was hungry. He was   9   to leave the restaurant when another man came in and put his hands on his stomach. And this sign was   10   enough for the waiter. In a few minutes, the waiter brought him a large plate of bread and meat. At last the Englishman had his meal in the same way.

1. A. nice	B. friendly	C. fine	D. well
2. A. eye	B. hand	C. mouth	D. arm
3. A. a little	B. few	C. a few	D. little
4. A. hungry	B. tired	C. sad	D. worried
5. A. washed	B. opened	C. closed	D. touched
6. A. dared	B. meant	C. had	D. decided
7. A. eat	B. drink	C. carry	D. play
8. A. happy	B. glad	C. sorry	D. afraid
9. A. quick	B. slow	C. ready	D. quiet
10. A. good	B. bad	C. bright	D. wrong

(十)

In China, very few children make pocket money.   1   , in western countries, most kids make pocket money by themselves. They make money in many different   2   .

When kids are very young, their parents help them sell the fruits of their own trees to neighbours. Kids may also help   3   do housework to make money at home. When they   4   sixteen, they can make money by sending newspapers or by working in fast food restaurants,   5   during the summer holidays.

There are many   6   of making pocket money by kids themselves. First of all, they learn the   7   of money by working hard so that they will not waste any. Secondly, they learn to   8   money to buy things they need or want, such as books, pencils, movies, and even clothes they like. Thirdly, they learn to   9   the daily life problems by helping their parents or others. Making pocket money is   10   for children when they grow up. That is why parents encourage their kids to make pocket money.

1. A. Also	B. Anyway	C. However	D. Besides
2. A. ways	B. levels	C. homes	D. countries
3. A. teachers	B. friends	C. parents	D. neighbors
4. A. get	B. have	C. catch	D. reach
5. A. really	B. hardly	C. properly	D. especially
6. A. choices	B. advantages	C. problems	D. lessons
7. A. fun	B. value	C. message	D. purpose
8. A. count	B. waste	C. manage	D. change
9. A. give up	B. look up	C. deal with	D. meet with
10. A. helpful	B. careful	C. beautiful	D. successful

第三节 阅读理解

根据教学大纲要求,应特别注意阅读能力的培养与训练。一般河北省高等职业院校单招英语阅读理解篇数为两篇,题材新颖,信息量大、覆盖面广,可读性和实用性强。考查内容主要为:

1. 理解主旨要求。

任何一段独立完整的材料都会有其主旨要义。有时从一开头就可以看出作者希望读者通过阅读本材料能够了解些什么,有时候则需要从文章的字里行间中推断出来。这类试题主要考查读者领会大意和归纳、概括的能力。

2. 理解文中具体信息。

为支撑所要阐述的主题,短文中会有大量的细节信息,能否准确掌握与理解这样一些细节,会关系到对全文主旨的把握。这类试题有时比较直接,理解字面意义即可答出,有时则较为间接,需要经过归纳概括和推理才能做出判断和选择。

3. 根据上下文推测生词的词义。

在阅读英语材料这类真实语言活动过程中,遇到生词本属正常,但我们并不是每次遇到生词就要去查词典。正确理解掌握阅读材料中单词或短语的含义是理解全文意思的基础。在阅读过程中根据上下文等背景条件推测词义也是现实语言活动中的一项重要技巧。需要指出的是,不应简单地将英语单词的词义等同于词典里所标注的汉语意思,需要根据具体语境把握词汇的确切含义才能真正地理解文意,这种不使用词典而通过上下文来推测词义的能力是语言运用能力中非常重要的一个部分。

4. 做出简单判断和推理。

阅读英语材料的主要目的是获取信息,在实际阅读活动中,有时需要根据文字中所提供的事实与线索经过一番逻辑推理,才能掌握作者虽未提及但确实存在或很可能发生的事情,这种推理判断能力在"阅读理解"中是不可或缺的。

5. 理解文章的基本结构。

为能比较准确、深刻地理解文章,必须对文章的结构有所了解。例如对说明文中主题句和主题段位置的认识判断等。这方面的考查涉及对所读文章中句与句、段与段之间的逻辑联系,也有对整篇文章的掌握能力,常可反映在某段大意或指代关系的题目中。

6. 理解作者的意图和态度。

每段语言材料都有其特定的写作目的,或为传递信息,或为愉悦读者,或为阐述某一道理,这些目的往往不一定直接用话语表达出来,而是隐含于字里行间。读者在整体理解文章内容的基础上才能领会作者的言外之意、弦外之音。

(一)

Mr. Smith is our Chinese teacher. He always asks the same student to answer his questions because he doesn't look at the students at all. Yesterday he questioned Dick three times. Dick was very angry. After class Dick asked me, "What shall I do?" I told him a good idea. Now we are having a Chinese class. Mr. Smith wants one of us to read the text. "Dick, please read the text." "Dick isn't here today." Dick stands up and says. "Oh, I see. you read it, please."

1. Mr. Smith teaches us _____ .
   A. English　　　　　B. Maths　　　　　C. Physics　　　　　D. Chinese
2. He always asks the same student to _____ .
   A. translate the text　　　　　B. read the text
   C. tell a story　　　　　D. answer his questions
3. Yesterday he questioned Dick _____ .
   A. once　　　　　B. twice　　　　　C. three times　　　　　D. four times
4. _____ told Dick a good idea.
   A. Tim　　　　　B. Mr. Smith　　　　　C. The writer　　　　　D. "I"
5. Is the idea really good? _____ .
   A. Yes, it is　　　B. No, it isn't　　　C. Yes, it does　　　D. No, it doesn't

(二)

Most people who work in the office have a boss（老板）. So do I（我也是）. But my boss is a little unusual. What's unusual about him? Many men have dogs, but few men bring their dogs to the office every day. My boss's dog, Robinson, is big and brown. My boss brings him to work every day. He takes the dog to meetings and he takes the dog to lunch. When there is telephone call for my boss, I always know if he is in the office. I only look under his desk. If I see something brown and hairy（毛茸茸的）under it, I know my boss is somewhere in the office. If there is no dog, I know my boss is out.

1. People _____ bring dogs to the office.
   A. usually　　　　　B. often　　　　　C. few　　　　　D. sometimes
2. My boss is Robinson's _____ .
   A. boss　　　　　B. master　　　　　C. classmate　　　　　D. teacher
3. Robinson goes to meetings _____ my boss.
   A. for　　　　　B. without　　　　　C. instead of（代替）　　　　　D. with
4. Robinson is always under the desk if the boss is _____ .
   A. in the office　　　B. at meetings　　　C. out of the office　　　D. out of work
5. The passage tells us the boss _____ the dog very much.
   A. looks like　　　B. hates（恨）　　　C. likes　　　D. trust（信任）

(三)

The earth moves round the sun, and the moon moves round the earth. When our part（部分）of the earth turns to the sun, it is day. When our part of the earth turns away from the sun, it is night.

The sun is much bigger than the moon. But sometimes the moon looks bigger than the sun, because it's much nearer to the earth.

The sun is very bright. It gives a very strong light. The moon looks quite bright, too. But it doesn't give any light at all. It reflects（反射）the sun's light.

The moon looks much bigger and brighter than the stars. But in fact the stars are much bigger and brighter than the moon. They look smaller than the moon because they're much farther away from us.

1. _____ moves round _____ .

    A. The earth, the moon   B. The moon, the earth

    C. The moon, the stars   D. The sun, the earth

2. Sometimes the moon looks bigger than the sun, because _____ .

    A. it is much bigger than the sun   B. it comes out only at night

    C. it is much nearer to the earth than the sun   D. it doesn't give a very strong light

3. The sun _____ .

    A. gives us light   B. gives more light than the moon does

    C. moves round the earth   D. makes the moon move round the earth

4. The stars _____ .

    A. look much bigger than the sun

    B. look much brighter than the moon

    C. are a lot brighter than the moon, but they are not bigger than the moon

    D. are much farther away from us than the moon

5. The moon looks bright because _____ .

    A. it gives light   B. it reflects (反射) the sun's light

    C. it is nearer to the earth   D. it is nearer to the sun

(四)

When people meet each other for the first time in Britain, they say "How do you do?" and shake hands (握手). Usually they do not shake hands when they just meet or say goodbye. But they shake hands after they haven't met for a long time or when they will be away from each other for a long time.

Last year a group of German students went to England for a holiday. Their teacher told them that the English people hardly shake hands. So when they met their English friends at the station, they kept their hands behind their backs. The English students had learned that the Germans shake hands as often as possible, so they put their hands in front and got ready to shake hands with them. It made both of them laugh.

1. It is _____ if you know the language and some of the customs of the country.

    A. not useful   B. not helpful   C. very helpful   D. very bad

2. English people usually shake hands when they _____ .

    A. meet every time   B. meet for the first time

    C. say goodbye to each other   D. say hello to each other

3. Usually English people don't shake hands _____ .

    A. when they will be away for a long time   B. when they say "How do you do?"

    C. when they just meet or say goodbye   D. after they haven't met for a long time

4. Which is right? _____

    A. German people shake hands as often as possible.

    B. English people like shaking hands very much.

C. German people hardly shake hands.

D. Neither English people nor Germans like shaking hands.

5. This story is about _____ .

  A. shaking hands   B. languages

  C. customs   D. languages and customs

（五）

  My name is Kate. Mr. Zhou is my father and I'm his daughter. My mother is an American, but my father is a Chinese. I have a brother. His name is Jim. We are studying in China now. Jim and I study in the same middle school, but in different grades. We go to school at seven in the morning and come back home after school in the afternoon. We have some Chinese friends. We love China.

1. How many people are there in Kate's family?

  A. 3.   B. 4.   C. 5.   D. 6.

2. Who is a Chinese in Kate's family?

  A. Kate's father.   B. Kate's mother.

  C. Kate's parents.   D. Kate's brother.

3. When do they go to school in the morning?

  A. At six thirty.   B. At seven.

  C. At seven ten.   D. At eight.

4. Jim and Kate are in _____ .

  A. different schools   B. the same school

  C. different grades   D. Both B and C

5. Kate and Jim have some Chinese _____ .

  A. fathers   B. mothers   C. friends   D. books

（六）

  Look! A nice watch is on the desk, and it is new. The colour of the watch is pink. It is a small watch for girls. What's the time on it? It's a quarter past ten. Whose is it? Let's ask Lucy. "Lucy, is this watch yours?" "Let me have a look. Yes, it is." "Put it on, please. You must look after your things." "Thank you very much, Jim."

1. The watch is _____ .

  A. old   B. new   C. black   D. white

2. The watch is a _____ watch.

  A. boy's   B. man's   C. girl's   D. woman's

3. The time on the watch is _____ .

  A. ten o'clock   B. ten thirty

  C. five to ten   D. ten fifteen

4. It's _____ watch.

  A. Lily's   B. my   C. Han Mei's   D. Lucy's

5. Who sees the watch?

  A. Nobody.   B. Jim.   C. Miss Gao.   D. I don't know.

（七）

　　Come here and look at these pictures. This is a picture of a man, Mr. Brown, and a boy, Richard Brown. Mr. Brown is Richard Brown's father. And Richard Brown is Mr. Brown's son. That is a picture of a woman, Mrs. Brown, and a girl, Mary Brown. Mrs. Brown is Mr. Brown's wife and Mary Brown's mother. Mary Brown is Richard's sister.

1. Mary's father is _____ .
   A. Richard   B. Richard Brown
   C. Mr. Richard   D. Mr. Brown
2. The mother of Richard is _____ .
   A. Mary   B. Miss Mary
   C. Mrs. Mary   D. Mrs. Brown
3. Richard Brown is _____ .
   A. Mary's sister   B. Richard's brother
   C. Mr. Brown's son   D. Mary's son
4. Mr. Brown's daughter is _____ .
   A. Richard's sister   B. the wife of Richard
   C. Richard's friend   D. Mrs. Brown
5. There are _____ people in the two pictures.
   A. eight   B. six   C. five   D. four

（八）

　　A man has a bird. It is very clever. Every day the man speaks to the bird. "Hello!" he says. "Hello!" the bird answers. "What are you doing?" says the man. "What are you doing?" says the bird.

　　The man is not at home one day. A thief comes in. He is taking many things. "Hello!" The thief hears the bird's words. "What are you doing?" The thief is very afraid, so he does not take any things and runs out of the house.

1. The man teaches the bird _____ .
   A. how to say something   B. how to sing songs
   C. how to eat something   D. how to dance
2. The bird is _____ .
   A. very nice   B. very clever
   C. very beautiful   D. very silly（傻的）
3. The man speaks to the bird _____ .
   A. sometimes   B. once a week
   C. every week   D. every day
4. The thief is taking _____ things.
   A. a few   B. a little   C. a lot of   D. some
5. The thief _____ out of the room.
   A. walks   B. comes   C. runs   D. goes

(九)

Channel 1	Channel 2
18：00 Around China	17：45 Computers today
18：30 Children's programme	18：10 Foreign arts
19：00 News	18：30 Morden English
19：30 Weather report	19：00 Animal world
19：40 Around the world	19：25 In Asia
20：10 TV play：sisters	20：20 Sports
21：00 English for today	21：00 Sports player：Yao Ming
21：15 Pop music	21：45 English news
21：55 Talk show	22：05 On TV next week

1. If you want to know something about Yao Ming, the best programme for you is _____.
   A. Talk show　　　　B. Sports　　　　C. Sports player　　　　D. TV play
2. You'll know about _____ at 19：00 on Channel 2.
   A. animals　　　　B. news　　　　C. foreign arts　　　　D. Asia
3. If you want to watch NBA, the best programme for you would be _____.
   A. Sports　　　　B. Around the world　　　　C. Foreign arts　　　　D. English news
4. If you like music very much, the best programme is _____.
   A. at 21：45 on Channel 2　　　　B. at 21：55 on Channel 1
   C. at 21：00 on Channel 2　　　　D. at 21：15 on Channel 1
5. "Morden English" is a programme that _____
   A. teaches you English
   B. tells you something about English classroom
   C. lets you know English news
   D. makes foreign friends

(十)

　　This is a true story. It happened to a friend of mine a year ago. While my friend, Peter, was reading in bed, two thieves（贼）climbed into another room. It was very dark, so they turned on the light. Suddenly they heard a voice behind them.

　　"What's up?" "What's up?" someone called.

　　The thieves turned off the light and ran away as quickly as they could. Peter heard the noise and came downstairs quickly. He turned on the light, but he couldn't see anyone. The thieves were already gone. But Peter's parrot, Henry, was still there.

　　"What's up, Peter?" He called.

　　"Nothing, Henry," Peter said and smiled, "go back to sleep."

1. It was very dark, so _____.
   A. the thieves turned off the light　　　　B. the thieves turned on the light

C. the thieves climbed into another room   D. the thieves heard a voice behind them
2. What happened when they turned on the light?
   A. They found a lot of money.   B. They heard a voice behind them.
   C. The police came in.   D. They entered the room.
3. What did they do when they heard a voice?
   A. They turned off the light.   B. They entered the room.
   C. They ran away as quickly as they could.   D. A and C
4. Who called "What's up"?
   A. Peter.   B. Peter's son, Henry.
   C. The thieves.   D. Peter's parrot, Henry.
5. Which is not true?
   A. It's a true story.   B. It happened two years ago.
   C. Peter was my friend.   D. The thieves ran away with nothing.

(十一)

I'm Tom. I'd like to say something about schools in my country. Schools begin in September after a long summer holiday. There are two terms in a school year; the first term is from September to January; and the second is from February to June. Most children begin to go to school when they are five years old. Most children are seventeen or eighteen years old when they finish high school.

High school students take only five or six subjects each term. They usually go to the same classroom every day, and they have homework for every class. After class, they do a lot of interesting things.

After high school, many students go to colleges. They usually have to pay a lot of money. So many college students work after class to get money for their studies.

1. In Tom's country, schools begin in _____ after a long summer holiday.
   A. September   B. July   C. May   D. February
2. When a boy is five years old, he _____.
   A. has to stay at home   B. can go to high school
   C. begins to go to school   D. always plays at home
3. In Tom's country, high school students _____ after class.
   A. do their homework   B. go to work
   C. play basketball   D. do a lot of interesting things
4. Many college students work after class to _____.
   A. help their parents   B. get money for their studies
   C. help others   D. learn some useful things
5. Which is right?
   A. The second term is from February to June.
   B. Students have three terms a year.
   C. A 6-year-old child usually has six subjects at school.
   D. Students don't like to go to schools.

（十二）

Movie	*Alice in Wonderland*《爱丽丝梦游仙境》	*Shrek Forever After*《怪物史莱克》	*Toy Story 3*《玩具总动员3》	*Harry Potter*（Ⅰ）《哈利·波特1》
Release date（上映日期）	March 5	May 21	June 18	November 19
Company（公司）	Walt Disney Pictures	Dream Work Animation	Disney·Pixar	Warner Bros. Pictures
Director（导演）	Tim Burton	Mike Mitchell	Lee Unkrich	David Yates
Extra Information（更多信息）	An extension of Lewis Carroll's original story	The 4th Shrek movie	A story about Andy and his toys	Part Two of the final movie to be released in 2011

1. You will see *Harry Potter*（Ⅰ）on _____ at the earliest.
   A. March 5　　　B. May 21　　　C. November 19　　　D. June 18
2. The movie made by Dream Work Animation is _____.
   A. *Toy Story 3*　　　　　　　　B. *Harry Potter*（Ⅰ）
   C. *Shrek Forever After*　　　　D. *Alice in Wonderland*
3. _____ directed *Alice in Wonderland*.
   A. David Yates　　　　　　　　B. Tim Burton
   C. Mike Mitchell　　　　　　　D. Lee Unkrich
4. Which of the movies is a story about Andy and his toys?
   A. *Toy Story 3*.　　　　　　　B. *Shrek Forever After*.
   C. *Alice in Wonderland*.　　　D. *Harry Potter*（Ⅰ）.
5. How many movies can you find in the table?
   A. Two.　　　B. Three.　　　C. Four.　　　D. Five.

（十三）

Xiao Shenyang was born in 1981 in Liaoning, China. He became famous after taking part in the CCTV Spring Festival Gala. He became a student of Zhao Benshan, a famous comedy actor, in 2006. He is good at Er Ren Zhuan, a popular folk（民间的）song-and-dance duet in northeast China. Many people enjoy his Er Ren Zhuan performances.

Can you find a ring in an egg? But Liu Qian, a well-known magician（魔术师）from Taiwan, China, found it in front of the audiences at 2009 CCTV Spring Festival Gala. Liu Qian was born in 1976. At the age of 12, he won Taiwan's Youth Magic Competition. To make his performance better, he often performed on streets, roads and other places for people.

	Jackie Chan was born on April 7, 1954. His parents called him "Chan Kong-sang", which means "born in Hong Kong." In the early 1980s, Jackie went to Hollywood. Today, he is well-known all over the world. Many people like his action movies very much.

1. When he was _____ years old, Xiao Shenyang became a student of Zhao Benshan.
   A. 23   B. 24   C. 25   D. 27
2. Where was Liu Qian born?
   A. In Liaoning Province.   B. In Taiwan.
   C. In Hong Kong.   D. In Beijing.
3. When did Liu Qian win Taiwan's Youth Magic Competition?
   A. In 1976.   B. In 1980.   C. In 1988.   D. In 2006.
4. Jackie Chan is a well-known _____.
   A. actor   B. magician   C. pianist   D. player
5. Which of the following is WRONG according to the passage?
   A. Zhao Benshan is a famous comedy actor.
   B. Xiao Shenyang is younger than Liu Qian.
   C. Jackie Chan was born in Hong Kong, China.
   D. Liu Qian performed in the street to make money.

(十四)

☺Letter 1
Whatever I do, I always think about if other people will like it. How can I stop worrying about what they think? —Eva, 14, Illinois
☺Letter 2
My dream is to be on the Olympic team for gymnastics. My dad thinks I started too late and I'll never be able to make it. He puts me down, but I want his support. What should I do? —Erica, 9, Texas
☺Letter 3
What should I do if I failed a test? I'm afraid to tell my mom because she might get mad at me and I can't play soccer. And soccer is like the world to me. —Ashley, 12, Wisconsin
☺Letter 4
I just moved and I'm kind of shy, so how do I make new friends? —Jessica, 11, Canada
Dr. Molly's Answer ①
You should tell him about your dream and that if you work really hard, it might happen even though you started late. The sooner you tell your dad how you feel, the sooner you'll be able to work on making your dream come true.

续表

Dr. Molly's Answer ②
Nobody knows you at your new school. You have nothing to lose, so gather up all your courage and go over to someone who looks friendly and introduce yourself. You can ask that person about your teacher or the other kids in your class to break the ice. Good luck!
Dr. Molly's Answer ③
It's better to tell your mom the truth than for her to find out another way. When you tell her, explain why you failed the test. Ask her if she can help you study in the future, so you'll do better on your tests and also have time for the soccer you love.
Dr. Molly's Answer ④
Just be yourself and try not to care about what others think. The more you think about it, the worse you will feel. Always act strong and confident. Even if you are a little unsure of something, don't doubt (怀疑) your abilities to do things right. Just relax.

1. Jessica _____ .
   A. wonders how to make new friends
   B. wishes to be on the Olympic team
   C. is afraid to tell her mom about her failing a test
   D. keeps worried about what other people think about her
2. _____ loves playing soccer best.
   A. Erica   B. Eva   C. Ashley   D. Jessica
3. Erica's dad doesn't support her because he thinks she _____ .
   A. is a little shy and can't do it well   B. didn't start at a very early age
   C. is too young to be on the team   D. doesn't work hard
4. According to Dr. Molly, Eva should _____ .
   A. hold on to her dream   B. always tell the truth
   C. be brave to say hello to others   D. be confident of herself
5. Which is the correct order of Dr. Molly's answers to the four letters?
   A. ①④③②   B. ③④②①   C. ②③①④   D. ④①③②

(十五)

Singapore's public transport system (公共交通系统) is one of the best in the world, so you should have no problem finding your way around like a local (当地人). There are three main forms of public transport that you would find in any other major city—trains, buses and taxis.

TRAINS

Trains run from 6 a.m. to midnight. Single trip tickets start at 80 cents. If you buy an EZ-Link card for $15, you can ride the trains and buses all you like.

If you need more information, just call Transit Link on 1-800-767-4333.

BUSES

There are several bus services in Singapore and fares (车费) start at 80 cents. Be sure to always ask the driver the cost of your ticket as he can not give changes.

If you need help, just call Transit Link on 1-800-767-4333.

TAXIS

There are three main taxi companies—City Cab (6552-2222), Comfort (6552-1111) and Tibs (6552-8888). Booking (预订) can also be made easily by calling the numbers listed above.

RENTAL (租) CARS

Driving in Singapore is a pleasure and if you like to travel at your own pace, renting a car is a good choice. Renting takes away the hassle of getting to places around Singapore. Just sit back and enjoy the city. It also means you'll get to see a lot more that a train or a bus won't let you see.

For car rental, call Avis on +65-6737-1668.

1. If you need to find the bus number, you may call _____.
   A. +65-6737-1668
   B. 6552-8888
   C. 1-800-767-4333
   D. 6552-2222

2. By an EZ-Link card, you can take _____.
   A. both buses and trains
   B. only trains
   C. both buses and taxis
   D. only rental cars

3. When you take a bus there, always remember to _____.
   A. take your own license with you
   B. ask the driver how much your ticket is
   C. buy the bus map of Singapore
   D. book your ticket ahead of time

4. What does the word "hassle" mean in Chinese?
   A. 麻烦。
   B. 乐趣。
   C. 景点。
   D. 费用。

5. What do you know about traveling in Singapore from the passage?
   A. A local has no trouble finding his way around.
   B. It's much cheaper to go around by bus than by train.
   C. You can see a lot more in Singapore only by renting a car.
   D. It's very convenient for visitors to travel in Singapore.

（十六）

Angel Is Having a Big Week Sale!	Harry Potter Magic Show
Everything 30% off All TVs radios, MP3s, digital cameras and computers 29 Zhongshan Street Open from 9:30 a.m. to 6:30 p.m.	See magic performances • The quiet bell • The clever boy • The terrible message Two hours Saturday morning, starts at 9:30 The Grand Cinema, 741 High Street
Cleaner Wanted	**Kite Museum**
Make a large house clean and tidy Paid at $20 a day Call us this evening 19:00 – 22:00 Tel: 2911 – 4788	8:30 – 17:30 from Thursday to Sunday Ticket: 20 yuan 22 Heping Road Tel: 6528 – 7211 Show you all kinds of kites!

1. Angel has MP3 at _____ off.
   A. 30%   B. 20%
   C. 10%   D. 5%
2. On Saturday morning, Harry Potter Magic Show will end at _____.
   A. 9:30   B. 10:00
   C. 11:00   D. 11:30
3. How much will the cleaner get a day?
   A. $10.   B. $20.
   C. $30.   D. $40.
4. George can visit Kite Museum _____.
   A. at 8:00   B. at 13:00
   C. at 18:00   D. at 20:00
5. The Kite Museum opens _____ days a week.
   A. 1   B. 2   C. 3   D. 4

（十七）

Huaihua Foreign Language School Li Nan, Teacher of English Yingfeng Street, Huaihua, China Tel: 0745 – 2709348 Fax: 0745 – 2709756 E-mail: Linan@21cn.com MP: 1240822018 Zip code: 418000	Daqing Children's Hospital Liu Hong, Doctor 12 Xingling Road, Changchun, Jilin 130027 Tel: 0431 – 5645972 13704358529 (mobile) Fax: 0431 – 5768904 E-mail: cclh@163.com

Red Star Farm Zhang Hui, Farmer Shangping Village, Zhejiang, 419100 Tel：0745－6826194 13973098479（mobile） MP：1270803706	Tiantai Taxi Company Yang Jun, Driver 235St. Tongzhi, Hangzhou, Zhejiang 31007 Tel：0571－7038385 Fax：0571－7065834 E-mail：hzyi@163.com MP：1992301636

1. We can learn English from _____.
   A. Yang Jun   B. Zhang Hui   C. Liu Hong   D. Li Nan
2. You may telephone _____ for help if your little sister is ill.
   A. Yang Jun   B. Zhang Hui
   C. Liu Hong   D. Li Nan
3. We can call _____ when we want to take a taxi to Hangzhou Railway Station.
   A. 13973098479   B. 0745－2709348
   C. 1992301636   D. 13704358529
4. Of the four, we can't send fax to the _____.
   A. driver   B. teacher   C. doctor   D. farmer
5. If you have some questions about your health, please send an E-mail to _____.
   A. Linan@21cn.com   B. cclh@163.com
   C. hzyi@163.com   D. hhmx@163.com

（十八）

One day, little Tom went to the shopping center with his parents. He saw a toy in a shop window. He liked it so much that he quickly walked into the shop. After looking at the toy for some time, he found he could not see his parents. He began to cry. A woman saw him crying and told him to wait at the gate. Five minutes later, he saw his parents were running to him.

His mother said, "How nice to see you again! Dad and I were very worried." Tom <u>promised</u> that this would never happen again.

1. Little Tom went to the shopping center with _____.
   A. his father and mother   B. his friends
   C. his sisters   D. his uncle
2. Tom saw _____ in a shop window.
   A. a bag   B. a book   C. a toy   D. a pen
3. Why did Tom begin to cry?
   A. He could not see his parents.   B. He could not get the toy.
   C. He could not find the way home.   D. He could not find his money.
4. _____ later, he saw his parents.
   A. 10 minutes   B. 8 minutes   C. 6 minutes   D. 5 minutes
5. What does "<u>promised</u>" mean?
   A. 请求。   B. 保证。   C. 哭泣。   D. 看到。

(十九)

Smith is an engineer working in a computer company. His family lives near the bus stop and a shopping center. They live in a house with 3 bedrooms and a big living room. The house is comfortable to live in.

However, in order to save time, he wants to exchange his house for a similar (相似的) one or even a little smaller one near his company.

If you are interested, please call him at 5543321.

1. What does Smith do?
    A. An actor.　　　　B. An engineer.　　　　C. A teacher.　　　　D. A student.
2. How many bedrooms are there in his house?
    A. 2.　　　　B. 3.　　　　C. 4.　　　　D. 5.
3. How is his house?
    A. Comfortable.　　　　B. Beautiful.　　　　C. Not good.　　　　D. Small.
4. He wants to exchange his house in order to _____.
    A. save time　　　　B. save money　　　　C. change his job　　　　D. go abroad
5. Which phone number is right?
    A. Five-five-four-four-three-three-one　　　　B. Five-five-four-three-three-two-one
    C. Five-five-four-two-three-three-one　　　　D. Five-five-four-three-three-three-one

(二十)

One day, Li Hua saw a picture on the wall. It is London Tea Trade Center. It is on the north bank of the River Thames. It is very important to drink tea in every day lives of the British people. Tea is the British national drink. Everyone has 4 cups of tea every day, or some 1,500 cups every year.

About 30% of the world's tea is sold to London, and Britain is the biggest importer (进口国) of tea in the world.

It is becoming more popular because it is good for health. In drinking tea, they feel very happy.

1. What did Li Hua see in the picture?
    A. London Museum.　　　　B. London Tea Trade Center.
    C. London Sports Center.　　　　D. London Bridge.
2. Where is London Tea Trade Center?
    A. On the south bank of the River Thames.　　　　B. On the west bank of the River Thames.
    C. On the north bank of the River Thames.　　　　D. On the east bank of the River Thames.
3. How many cups of tea does everyone drink a year?
    A. 1,400.　　　　B. 1,500.　　　　C. 1,600.　　　　D. 1,700.
4. _____ is the biggest importer of tea in the world.
    A. Britain　　　　B. China　　　　C. America　　　　D. Japan
5. It is becoming more popular because it is _____.
    A. good for taste　　　　B. good for smell
    C. good for health　　　　D. good for sleeping

第三章 模拟测试

模拟测试（一）

一、词汇和语法（共10小题；每小题2分，满分20分）

从每题所给的四个选项中，选出最佳答案，将其序号在答题卡相应位置涂黑。

1. I won't go _____ he comes back.
   A. until   B. while   C. when   D. why

2. —Which is your new English teacher?
   —The young lady _____ red over there.
   A. with   B. in   C. on   D. for

3. The traffic on this road is much _____ than before, isn't it?
   A. good   B. better   C. best   D. worse

4. Where's Tom? His mother _____ him now.
   A. is looking for   B. will look for
   C. has looked for   D. looks for

5. It's dangerous _____ it while crossing the street.
   A. answering   B. answer
   C. to answer   D. answers

6. —Sonia, is this your dictionary?
   —No, it's not _____.
   A. my   B. me   C. mine   D. I

7. More and more young people go swimming _____ summer.
   A. at   B. in   C. on   D. to

8. The boy is sleeping. Please _____ the radio.
   A. turn up   B. turn down   C. turn on   D. turn around

9. Mom is making dinner. It _____ so nice!
   A. smells   B. tastes   C. feels   D. sounds

10. Do you think _____ necessary to learn English well?
    A. it   B. one   C. its   D. itself

二、阅读理解（共 10 小题；每小题 3 分，满分 30 分）

阅读下面两篇短文，从每题所给的四个选项中，选出最佳答案，将其序号在答题卡相应位置涂黑。

A

One day Jack's wife was cleaning out a closet（壁橱）.

"Look at all these umbrellas（雨伞）," she said to Jack. "There are eight and they are all broken."

"I'll take them to the umbrella shop and have them mended（修理）," Jack said.

Jack took the eight umbrellas to the shop and left them there. "They'll be ready tomorrow," the shopkeeper said.

That evening Jack went home from the office by bus as usual. He sat next to an old woman. She had an umbrella on the floor near her.

When the bus reached his stop, he picked up her umbrella and stood up. "Hey!" the woman said. "That's my umbrella!"

"I'm sorry," Jack said, and at the same time he gave the umbrella to her. "I wasn't thinking. Please excuse me."

The next day he got back the umbrellas from the umbrella shop and got on the bus.

As he sat down, a voice behind him said, "You certainly have a successful day!"

He turned around and saw the woman whose umbrella had almost been taken by him the day before.

11. Jack's wife found _____ umbrellas in the closet.
    A. eight broken   B. broken eight   C. eight new   D. new eight

12. _____ had the broken umbrellas mended in the umbrella shop.
    A. Jack's wife   B. Jack
    C. The shopkeeper   D. The old woman

13. That evening the old woman's umbrella was almost taken by _____.
    A. the shopkeeper B. Jack's wife   C. Jack   D. the driver

14. The next day Jack saw the woman _____.
    A. in the shop   B. at home   C. on the train   D. on the bus

15. Which of the following is True?
    A. Jack had an umbrella shop.
    B. The woman's umbrella was Jack's.
    C. The woman thought Jack was a thief.
    D. Jack bought eight umbrellas from the shop again.

B

Where is Love（爱）? How can we find Love?

Once a little boy wanted to meet Love. He knew it was a long trip to where Love lived, so he got his things ready with some pizzas（比萨饼）and drinks and started off. When he passed three streets, he saw an old woman sitting in the park and watching some birds. She looked very hungry. The boy gave her a pizza. She took it and smiled at him. The smile was so beautiful that he wanted to see it again, so he gave her a Coke (可乐). She smiled once again. The boy was very happy.

They sat there all the afternoon, eating and smiling, but they said nothing. When it grew dark, the boy decided to leave. But before he had gone more than a few steps, he turned around, ran back to the old woman and gave her a hug (拥抱). The woman gave him her biggest smile ever.

When the boy opened the door of his house, his mother was surprised by the look of joy (快乐) on his face and asked what had made him so happy. "I had lunch with Love. She has got the most beautiful smile in the world."

If the world is full of love, we can enjoy a better life.

16. When the little boy saw the old woman, she was _____.
    A. looking for a seat in the park   B. passing the street
    C. looking at some birds   D. having a pizza
17. The little boy gave the old woman a Coke because _____.
    A. the old woman still felt hungry   B. he wanted to see the smile again
    C. he didn't like the drink   D. the old woman paid him for it
18. The old woman gave the little boy the biggest smile _____.
    A. after the little boy went home   B. before it grew dark
    C. when she was drinking Coke   D. after the little boy hugged her
19. The boy's mother was surprised to see her son was very _____ when the door opened.
    A. happy   B. sad   C. unhappy   D. angry
20. Which of the following is TRUE?
    A. The little boy failed to find Love.
    B. Both the little boy and the old woman found what they wanted at last.
    C. The little boy decided never to go home.
    D. The old woman gave the little boy a hug to thank him.
    D. All the mosquitoes don't like to bite people for blood.

三、完形填空（共 **10** 小题；每小题 **3** 分，满分 **30** 分）

Friends are very important in people's lives. Some friends have __21__ interests (兴趣), and __22__ like the same things. Should friends be different __23__ same? In my opinion, I don't care. I have two best friends, Wang Lei and Lin Ying. Wang Lei __24__ like me. I am __25__ than most of the students in my class, and Wang Lei is also quiet. And we both enjoy __26__. On weekends, we often go to the library to do some reading. But the other friend of mine, Lin Ying, is __27__ different from me. She is much more outgoing, and she likes __28__ and often makes me laugh. She also likes __29__, so she is more healthy. I don't think differences are important in a __30__. What's your opinion?

21. A. same   B. different   C. active   D. free
22. A. others   B. another   C. other   D. the other

23. A. and	B. but	C. or	D. then
24. A. isn't	B. doesn't	C. does	D. is
25. A. quiet	B. quieter	C. outgoing	D. more outgoing
26. A. reading books	B. playing games		
C. watching TV	D. going to the movies		
27. A. not	B. more	C. quite	D. lots of
28. A. doing sports	B. telling jokes		
C. going to parties	D. going shopping		
29. A. sports	B. books	C. movies	D. subjects
30. A. match	B. concert	C. family	D. friendship

四、书面表达（满分 20 分）

31. 请以"My sister"为题，写一篇短文，把她的情况提前介绍给同学们。具体内容应包括：家庭情况、性格特点和兴趣爱好等。

要求：(1) 文章中不得出现真实的人名、校名和地名。

(2) 词数：100 词左右。

模拟测试（二）

一、单项选择题（每小题 2 分，共 40 分）

( ) 1. _____ late again, Bill!
　　A. Don't to be　B. Don't be　　　C. Not be　　　D. Be not

( ) 2. There _____ some eggs and cakes on the plate.
　　A. is　　　B. are　　　C. was　　　D. were

( ) 3. She has _____ orange skirt. _____ skirt is nice.
　　A. a; The　B. an; The　C. an; a　　D. the; The

( ) 4. Now Tom _____ a book about America.
　　A. writes　　　　　　B. has written
　　C. wrote　　　　　　D. is writing

( ) 5. —_____ do you sleep every day, Eric?
　　—For about eight hours.
　　A. How much　　　　B. How fast
　　C. How often　　　　D. How long

( ) 6. Would you like _____ to drink?
　　A. something　　　　B. anything
　　C. nothing　　　　　D. everything

( ) 7. This isn't my T-shirt. _____ is blue.
　　A. I　　　B. Me　　　C. Mine　　　D. My

(　　) 8. I _____ like playing volleyball.
　　　　A. don't　　　B. not　　　　　　C. am not　　　　　　D. doesn't

(　　) 9. Look! An old man is crossing the road. Let's go and help _____.
　　　　A. he　　　　B. him　　　　　　C. she　　　　　　　D. her

(　　) 10. —Are there any apples in the shop?
　　　　　—_____.
　　　　A. Yes, there is.　　　　　　　B. No, there isn't.
　　　　C. No, there aren't.　　　　　　D. Yes, there aren't.

(　　) 11. —When _____ school begin?
　　　　　—Next Monday.
　　　　A. has　　　B. does　　　　　　C. did　　　　　　　D. is going to

(　　) 12. We won't go unless you _____ soon.
　　　　A. had come　B. came　　　　　C. will come　　　　　D. come

(　　) 13. Jimmy and his parents visited us _____ a cold night last winter.
　　　　A. at　　　　B. in　　　　　　　C. of　　　　　　　　D. on

(　　) 14. Tina is as _____ as her sister, Tara.
　　　　A. outgoing　　　　　　　　　　B. more outgoing
　　　　C. the most outgoing　　　　　　D. the more outgoing

(　　) 15. —Where is Tom?
　　　　　—He _____ the USA. He _____ back in two months.
　　　　A. has gone to; comes　　　　　B. has bee to; will be
　　　　C. has been to; comes　　　　　D. has gone to; will be

(　　) 16. _____ Li Ming and Li Jun are teachers and they work in the same school.
　　　　A. Some　　B. Any　　　　　　C. Both　　　　　　　D. All

(　　) 17. Dave's father gave him _____ money for the school trip.
　　　　A. few　　　B. many　　　　　　C. some　　　　　　　D. any

(　　) 18. _____ people come to Beijing to visit the Great Wall every day.
　　　　A. Thousands of　　　　　　　　B. Thousand of
　　　　C. Thousands　　　　　　　　　D. Thousand

(　　) 19. What _____ is!
　　　　A. the clever monkey it　　　　　B. a clever monkey it
　　　　C. the clever monkey　　　　　　D. a clever monkey

(　　) 20. I think _____ a good habit to get up early.
　　　　A. this　　　B. it　　　　　　　C. that　　　　　　　D. its

二、请选出句子的答语选项（每小题2分，共20分）

A

(　　) 21. Can you dance?　　　　　　　A. Hangzhou.
(　　) 22. What day is it today?　　　　　B. Yes, please.

( ) 23. Would you like some beef?　　　C. They're eating some bananas.
( ) 24. What are the monkeys doing?　　D. It's Saturday.
( ) 25. Where's he from?　　　　　　　E. Yes, I can.

B

( ) 26. Do you speak English?　　　　　A. This is Tom.
( ) 27. What can I do for you?　　　　　B. I'd like to buy some eggs.
( ) 28. Let me help you.　　　　　　　　C. Yes, it is.
( ) 29. Who's that, please?　　　　　　　D. It's very kind of you.
( ) 30. It's really cold today, isn't it?　　E. Only a little.

三、阅读下面两组句子，给它们排序（每小题 2 分，共 20 分）

A

A：I'm going to travel to Beijing.
B：Where are you going to spend your summer holiday this year?
C：I'm going to get there by plane. Would you like to go with me?
D：Yes, I'd love to.
E：How are you going to get there?

31	32	33	34	35

B

A：Yes?
B：This afternoon.
C：Excuse me, Lin Tao!
D：My bike is broken. Can I borrow yours?
E：Certainly. When do you want it?

36	37	38	39	40

四、阅读下列短文，从每题所给的 A，B，C，D 四个选项中选出最恰当的答案（每小题 2 分，共 10 分）

　　Kate and Peter like sports. In summer they swim and in winter they skate. They are planning a skate trip for this weekend, but they don't know about the weather. It's 7∶30 now and they are listening to the weather report on the radio. The weather is giving the weather for the weekend.

　　"Friday is going to be cold and cloudy, but it's not going to rain. The temperature is going to be below zero. It's going to snow on Friday evening. Saturday and Sunday are going to be cold and sunny."

Now Kate and Peter are happy. The weather is going to be very nice for a skate trip. They are going to have a good time on the hills.

( ) 41. Kate and Peter like _____ .
   A. listening to the radio   B. watching TV
   C. sports   D. music

( ) 42. They are planning _____ for this weekend.
   A. a class meeting   B. a party
   C. a game   D. a skate trip

( ) 43. They want to know about _____ .
   A. the rain   B. the food
   C. the weather   D. the radio

( ) 44. It _____ on Saturday and Sunday.
   A. will rain   B. will be windy
   C. will be cloudy   D. will be cold and sunny

( ) 45. Kate and Peter are happy because _____ .
   A. the weather is going to be nice for a skate trip
   B. They are going to visit the friends
   C. They are going to see their parents
   D. They are going to have a good meal

五、请从方框中选择正确的选项补全对话（每小题 2 分，共 10 分）

Jane：Can I help you?
Li Ming：__46__
Jane：Let me see. One lady's skirt and one man's coat.
Li Ming：__47__
Jane：Is next Thursday soon enough?
Li Ming：__48__
Jane：Until 6：30 pm, sir.
Li Ming：__49__
Jane：Here's your receipt（收据）, sir.
Li Ming：__50__

A. When will they be ready?
B. I want to have these clothes cleaned.
C. Good．Thank you.
D. How much is it?
E. Well．Yes．When does the shop close?

模拟测试（三）

一、单项选择（每小题 2 分，共 20 分）

从每小题的四个选项中选出一个能填入题中相应空白处的最佳答案。

1. The museum is quite far. It will take you half _____ hour to get there by _____ bus.
   A. an; /   B. an; a   C. a; /   D. /; /

2. _____ are in the same class; _____ school is very big.
   A. We; ours   B. We; our   C. Our; we   D. Our; us

3. The mother told her son _____ the window.
   A. open   B. opening   C. to open   D. opened

4. I _____ my room last Sunday.
   A. clean   B. cleaning   C. am cleaning   D. cleaned

5. I'll be very busy _____ Friday afternoon.
   A. in   B. on   C. at   D. with

6. This kind of coffee is _____ than the other.
   A. better   B. good   C. best   D. well

7. —What did your mother say to you just now?
   —She asked _____ .
   A. where did I find the book   B. where I found the book
   C. where do I find the book   D. where I find the book

8. If he _____ to college, he will learn more.
   A. go   B. went   C. will go   D. goes

9. _____ sunny day it is! Let's go out for a walk.
   A. How   B. How a   C. What a   D. What

10. The man _____ is standing behind the counter is my brother.
    A. which   B. who   C. Whom   D. how

二、匹配（每小题 2 分，共 20 分）

Part 1（从 B 栏中找出 A 栏中单词的正确变化形式）

A	B
11. foot	A. him
12. he	B. farther
13. write	C. feet
14. far	D. singer
15. sing	E. written

Part 2（从 B 栏中找出 A 栏中单词的正确英文解释）

A	B
16. www	A. a place where students study
17. enjoy	B. anyone
18. school	C. World Wide Web
19. visit	D. like
20. anybody	E. pay a visit to

三、阅读理解（每小题 3 分，共 30 分）

根据所给阅读材料从下面每小题的四个选项中，选出一个能完成句子或回答所提问题的正确答案。

A

I have a large family. I have two brothers and two sisters. I am in the middle. Two brothers are older than me. Two sisters are younger than me. I go to school and I am in the sixth grade. I like my teachers and my teachers like me, too. My favorite class is music. I like music because music can make me happy. I have many friends, and my best friend is Bobby. Bobby and I do many things together. We swim together and play basketball together. On weekends we all go to the movies. We tell jokes and laugh. Life is great.

21. How many children are there in the boy's family?
    A. Three.　　　　B. Four.　　　　C. Five.　　　　D. Six.
22. What is the boy's favorite class?
    A. English.　　　B. History.　　　C. Music.　　　D. PE.
23. What sports do the boy and his friends like?
    A. Swimming.　　　　　　　　　B. Playing basketball.
    C. Playing football.　　　　　　D. Both A and B.
24. What will the boy and his friends do on weekends?
    A. Go to the movies.　　　　　B. Go shopping.
    C. Go to school.　　　　　　　D. Go fishing.
25. What is life like for the boy?
    A. It is great.　　　　　　　　B. It is just so-so.
    C. It is terrible.　　　　　　　D. It's boring.

B

John's Schedule

Monday	10:30 – 11:00 am	visit Uncle Peter in General Hospital
Tuesday	2:00 – 4:00 pm	swimming class
Wednesday	12:00 – 6:00 pm	part-time job（兼职工作）
Thursday	10:30 – 11:30 am	appointment（约会）with Mr. Green

Friday	11:00 am	go to the airport to meet Sam
Saturday	10:00 – 12:00 am	meet Dave to study for test
Sunday	5:00 – 7:00 pm	birthday party for Kate

26. _____ is ill in hospital.
    A. Kate   B. Peter   C. John   D. Sam
27. John has a swimming class on _____.
    A. Sunday   B. Tuesday   C. Wednesday   D. Thursday
28. John does his part-time job for _____ hours a week.
    A. five   B. six   C. ten   D. eleven
29. John meets Sam _____.
    A. at Dave's house   B. in the hospital
    C. at the airport   D. in Kate's home
30. Kate's birthday party is from _____ to _____ pm.
    A. 2:00; 4:00   B. 12:00; 6:00   C. 12:00; 5:00   D. 5:00; 7:00

四、判断正误（阅读下面的短文，正确的涂 T，错误的涂 F）（每小题 3 分，共 15 分）

Many people like traveling for their holidays. They go to hills, beaches, or forests. Some people like history, so they like visiting old and interesting places. In many countries, the travel agencies（旅行社）help you plan your holiday. You tell them what kind of places you like, how much money you want to spend, and they give you a lot of information（信息）about where to go, how to get there, where to stay, and what kind of activities you can do there. One of the holiday trips is called a package trip, That is, you just pay the money, and the travel agent will plan everything for you—the ticket for the train or plane, the hotel, the activities, and so on.

36. Few people go to hills, beaches, or forests for their holidays.
37. Some people like history and thus like going to old and interesting places.
38. The travel agencies will help you plan your holidays.
39. A package trip is traveling with a large backpack.
40. Pay the money, and the travel agent will plan everything for you.

五、写作（从下面两题中任选一题作答，共 15 分）

A. 根据给出的信息填写下面的空格。

In early 2021, the COVID-19 spread in Hebei. I saw a news report on TV. A nurse's mother got sick and was sent to hospital, but she was very busy with her job. She chose to work in her hospital. Every day she looked after the patients who got COVID-19. She couldn't look after her own mother.

In the hospital, all the doctors and nurses were warm-hearted and friendly. They did their best to save those patients. I was deeply moved. From that moment, I made up my mind to become a nurse to take care of my patients better.

  That's why I want to go to college. Although it is very hard to become an excellent nurse in China, still I will try to make my dream come true.

36. A nurse's mother got sick and _____.
37. Every day the nurse looked after _____.
38. All the doctors and nurses were _____.
39. I made up my mind to _____.
40. I will try to _____.

B. 请用英文写一篇题为"My Hometown"的作文，不少于60个词。

参考答案

第一章 基础知识

第一节 名词
1-5 DBBCC   6-10 BBCBB   11-15 CCACC   16-20 ABACB

第二节 冠词
1-5 BAACA   6-10 BCBDA   11-15 CDADD   16-20 ADCDA

第三节 代词
1-5 BADBB   6-10 ACBAD   11-15 ABCCC   16-20 AABBC
21-25 ACCDB   26-30 BCCBA

第四节 形容词
1-5 BCCBB   6-10 BDDCB   11-15 ACBBD   16-20 BDBCB

第五节 副词
1-5 BCDAD   6-10 ABBBA   11-15 ACBAD   16-20 BADCB

第六节 数词
1-5 CCBAA   6-10 DACAA   11-15 BDACD   16-20 ACABC

第七节 介词
1-5 BACBA   6-10 CDBDB   11-15 BABCC   16-20 CABBB

第八节 连词
1-5 ACCCC   6-10 AABBD   11-15 AACAD   16-20 DAABA

第九节 动词
1-5 CBAAD   6-10 BCCDA   11-15 CBCCC   16-20 CBDDD

第十节 动词时态
1-5 CBBAB   6-10 ADDBD   11-15 CDBBD   16-20 AAABD
21-25 CABDA   26-30 CDDCC   31-35 DABCD   36-40 DDCAD

第十一节 动词语态
1-5 BDDCC   6-10 BBAAC   11-15 BADAA   16-20 BABDB

第十二节 非谓语动词
1-5 DCDBD   6-10 CACDA   11-15 BACAD   16-20 ABBBA

第十三节 英语句子的基本句型
1-5 BABCA   6-10 DBCAC   11-15 CACAD   16-20 ACADB

第十四节 状语从句
1 – 5 ABCDB 6 – 10 BDDBB 11 – 15 BBABA 16 – 20 CABAD
21 – 25 ACDDC 26 – 30 DBDBB 31 – 35 BCDBB 36 – 40 CBCCD

第十五节 名词性从句
1 – 5 BCADD 6 – 10 CABAB 11 – 15 DCACC 16 – 20 ACBDC

第十六节 定语从句
1 – 5 BCBDD 6 – 10 ACADC 11 – 15 DDBCD 16 – 20 DDCAA

第十七节 感叹句
1 – 5 BDACA 6 – 10 AACDA 11 – 15 CDDDB 16 – 20 AADCD

第十八节 倒装句
1 – 5 ABDCB 6 – 10 BDCCB 11 – 15 BBBAD 16 – 20 ADBCD

第十九节 主谓一致
1 – 5 BABAD 6 – 10 ABCDA 11 – 15 BBCDA 16 – 20 BABAD
21 – 25 BABAA 26 – 30 CDBDB 31 – 35 CDABA

第二章 专项练习

第一节 日常交际用语
1 – 5 ACACC 6 – 10 DBDCA 11 – 15 ABCAC 16 – 20 DDABB
21 – 25 BDDBD 26 – 30 DABCB

第二节 完形填空
（一）1 – 5 CDAAC 6 – 10 DDABA （二）1 – 5 DBCBA 6 – 10 DABDC
（三）1 – 5 ADCBD 6 – 10 ACBBA （四）1 – 5 DCADB 6 – 10 BCDBA
（五）1 – 5 ABBCD 6 – 10 ACCDB （六）1 – 5 ACADD 6 – 10 CBCDA
（七）1 – 5 CBBDA 6 – 10 CDDBA （八）1 – 5 AABBA 6 – 10 ABCDD
（九）1 – 5 BCDAB 6 – 10 BBCCA （十）1 – 5 CACDD 6 – 10 BBCCA

第三节 阅读理解
（一）1 – 5 DDCDB （二）1 – 5 CBDAC （三）1 – 5 BCADB
（四）1 – 5 CBCAA （五）1 – 5 BABDC （六）1 – 5 BCDDB
（七）1 – 5 CDCAD （八）1 – 5 ABDCC （九）1 – 5 CAADA
（十）1 – 5 BBDDB （十一）1 – 5 ACDBA （十二）1 – 5 CCBAC
（十三）1 – 5 CBCAD （十四）1 – 5 ACBDD （十五）1 – 5 CABAD
（十六）1 – 5 ADBBD （十七）1 – 5 DCCDB （十八）1 – 5 ACADB
（十九）1 – 5 BBAAB （二十）1 – 5 BCBAC

第三章 模拟测试

模拟测试（一）

一、词汇和语法
1 – 5 ABBAC   6 – 10 CBBAA
二、阅读理解
11 – 15 ACCDB   16 – 20 CBDAB
三、完形填空
21 – 25 BACDB   26 – 30 ACBAD
四、书面表达
（略）

模拟测试（二）

一、单项选择题
1 – 5 BBBDD   6 – 10 ACABC   11 – 15 BDDAD   16 – 20 CCABB
二、请选出句子的答语选项
21 – 25 EDBCA   26 – 30 EBDAC
三、阅读下面两组句子，给它们排序
31 – 35 BAECD   36 – 40 CADEB
四、阅读下列短文，从每题所给的 A，B，C，D 四个选项中选出最恰当的答案
41 – 45 CDCDA
五、请从方框中选择正确的选项补全对话
46 – 50 BAEDC

模拟测试（三）

一、单项选择
1 – 5 ABCDB   6 – 10 ABDCB
二、匹配
Part 1（从 B 栏中找出 A 栏中单词的正确变化形式）
11 – 15 CAEBD
Part 2（从 B 栏中找出 A 栏中单词的正确英文解释）
16 – 20 CDAEB
三、阅读理解
21 – 25 CCDAA   26 – 30 BBBCD
四、判断正误
31 – 35 FTTFT

五、写作

A. 根据给出的信息填写下面的空格。

36. was sent to hospital

37. the patients who got COVID – 19

38. warm-hearted and friendly

39. become a nurse to take care of my patients better

40. make my dream come true

B. 请用英文写一篇题为"My Hometown"的作文，不少于60个词。（略）